I0467923

NO FEAR: TALES OF A CHANGE AGENT

OR

WHY I COULDN'T FIX NORTEL NETWORKS!

A Business Memoir
Tim Dempsey

This book is an original work and I, Timothy F. Dempsey, am the sole owner of its content. I have tried to recreate events, locales and conversations from my memories of them. When I use quotation marks attributed to others, this is to signify that this is my best *recollection* of what was said. I have carefully researched all sources and have made every effort to ensure that the information in this book is accurate. I do not assume responsibility and hereby disclaim any liability to any party for any loss, damage, or disruption caused, whether directly or indirectly, by errors or omissions, whether such errors or omissions result from negligence, accident, or any other cause. Any slights of people or organizations are unintentional. Potential purchasers who do not agree with the above caveats in this disclaimer are directed not to purchase the book or utilize the information.

Copyright © 2014 Timothy F. Dempsey
All rights reserved.

ISBN: 1500459607
ISBN 13: 9781500459604

DEDICATION

To all of the amazing people who worked in all the groups formerly known as OD—
You know who you are!

TABLE OF CONTENTS

Preface: La Costa, September, 2000   vii

Part 1: BUILDING CAPABILITY   1

Chapter 1: Welcome!   3
Chapter 2: You Can't Get There From Here   13
Chapter 3: Money's For Nothin'   23
Chapter 4: "Hr Has No Integrity"   31
Chapter 5: Rate This!   41
Chapter 6: Growin' Up   49

Part 2: ADDING VALUE   65

Chapter 7: Telecommunications Act Of 1996   67
Chapter 8: Nom Is A Dirty Word   73
Chapter 9: 90-Day Wonder   95
Chapter 10: Accountability   101
Chapter 11: Customer First   113
Chapter 12: "I Want To Change The Culture"   121
Chapter 13: Employee And Organization Learning   143
Chapter 14: House Rules   155
Chapter 15: Time To…Leave?   165

Part 3: LEARNING   177

Chapter 16: "It's About Leadership, Stupid!"   179
Chapter 17: Learnings & Judgments: Cleaning Up After
The Elephants Dance   193

EPILOGUE   213

ACKNOWLEDGMENTS   219

BIBLIOGRAPHY   221

PREFACE

Nortel Networks Executive Leadership Forum:
Moving to the Next Level: Let's Get on with It
La Costa, San Diego, California September 10–14, 2000

I arrived early on a Saturday morning at the end of September, 2000, giving myself time to assure that the site was ready and to explore my way around it. As usual, I would be in constant, continuous motion once the conference started, and I had learned the importance of knowing the quickest routes around the sprawling complex that would have groups of senior executives ensconced in pockets here and there.

I had mixed emotions, a little guilt, and maybe some bitterness from having to miss yet another entire weekend with my family, combined with excitement about the changes going on in the company and my role facilitating them. Nortel was soaring: $30 billion in sales and over 100,000 employees.

I was a little nervous. When I taught Organization Development (OD) to human resource (HR) professionals, I had a few caveats that I would badger them with, over and over. "Who's the client?" being one of the most prevalent. For a number of years, my client had been John Roth, whose coattails swept me along as he rose in the company, who had now been CEO for a few years. John had always been very clear about what he wanted out of an event and how he expected me to help him get it. Historically, these types of events were intended to rally the executives around some change initiative, often signaling a change in strategic direction. They would help get alignment to create the change. Most recently, John had been the sponsor, the host, and, for me, "the client." I would sometimes emcee, but I also had a gearbox role, making sure that all the parts were moving smoothly and that communications were flowing in real time. I had learned, for example, to build a lot of "white space" into the agenda, as much of the most important work happened during the breaks in hallways, restaurants, bars, and washrooms.

But things were changing. Clarence Chandran had become chief operating officer, and he was going to be the official sponsor and host of this conference, even though John was still pulling my puppet strings. In my mind, this was a sort of coming out party for Clarence. He wanted to celebrate the company's success, and he wanted the executives to enjoy themselves. He had encouraged us to bring our spouses, something that had not occurred before, at least not during my tenure.

I did not even consider bringing Janis, knowing that she would hate it, hate leaving the kids with a sitter for so long, and that I would have zero time to spend with her, as I typically worked eighteen-to-twenty-hour days at these events. I was surprised to learn from several executives that they had brought their spouses grudgingly—they didn't know they were allowed to say no.

Clarence, as always, did a superb job opening the conference, highlighting the good news of who we had become as a company and how the future was wide open. He thanked the executives who had brought their spouses, who would be free to enjoy the world-class spa while the executives worked. We were all excited about the prospect of being entertained during a gala evening that included Penn and Teller. I was personally delighted that I would get to meet our keynote speaker, the management guru Peter Drucker.

This conference had some of the trappings of a sales conference, I thought, rather than a strategic planning conference, but I was not anxious about it. Honestly, I, too, was caught up in the moment, proud of my influential role in the company, secretly hoping to be honored one of these years with the prestigious "Spirit of Nortel" award. I was extremely smug to be associated with John Roth, especially when he was given a rousing standing ovation as he was thanked for his tremendous success.

It wasn't until the middle of the first workday that I began to worry. The execs had been divided into six work groups each led by a very senior person. My role was to wander around, touch base with each team, see if they needed anything, and assure they were on track. First one, then two, then three different teams asked me if I could stay with them the whole day. During the lunch break, I talked with two of the leaders of those teams privately. I was trying to ascertain what was going on. "I want to make sure that we get the right answer. I want to make sure that my team pleases Clarence and John." Oh, shit! And they thought I could make it happen!

Those who are the most anxious seem to stay up the latest, and I was getting earfuls of fear while sipping Sambuca at two o'clock in the morning. My own fear meter started to rise about the third or fourth time I heard, "You gotta tell John."

"Tell John what, exactly?"

"The marketing numbers aren't real."

"What's fake, exactly?"

"Peel the layers and you'll see that the assumptions are that end-users will buy networks from each of our customers. End-users only need one network each. All the numbers are inflated."

"John's not going to listen to me. You report to him."

"Not anymore. I report to Clarence now."

"Well, then tell him." Really, I had this conversation several times that night. With very senior people that I trusted, admired, and respected.

Again, when I teach OD, I teach flexibility, adaptability when facilitating meetings or events: "Do what the people in the room need you to do, not what you had planned to do in advance." But I was unsure what to do with this data. I had not set the agenda, and I knew I could not arbitrarily alter it. I decided, after tossing and turning late that night, that coaching the executives to tell their bosses about any concerns was exactly what the limit of my role was.

It was coming up to five o'clock on the day of the big gala. Spouses were invited, expecting to attend, most of them excited about it. Execs had been promised that we would be done at five o'clock, to have an hour to spend with their spouses to get ready. Last on the agenda was an external consultant, one that I had not yet met. He was going to present a change model.

The guy was professional: smart, articulate, and organized. He presented well. But he was victimized by the situation, starting just a few minutes before five, and opening with, "I know you are supposed to be done by five, but this will just take a few minutes; I just have a couple of charts. He was at least ten or fifteen charts in when I looked at the clock and saw five twenty. As I paced in the back of the room like a caged tiger, one by one, senior execs, friends of mine, the ones I most trusted and respected, began trapping me, cornering me, basically asking the same question: "What the fuck is going on?"

I got defensive: "It's not my fault!"

Finally he was finished, somewhere around five thirty, and I was surprised to hear Clarence say, "Tim Dempsey will now close out today's session and tell you what's happening tonight."

I was not on the agenda, had not prepared for this. But, I was usually decent enough on my feet and certainly this type of surprise had happened many times before. As I climbed the stairs to the stage, I sort of turned to the execs and said, "Don't worry, I only have a few charts…" The audience cracked up, and I felt that I had done a good job of relieving the tension and diffusing some of the anger.

As I traversed the ten feet to the lectern, Clarence very gently leaned over to me and whispered, "That was a low blow, Tim. I expect better from you." I imagine the blood drained from my face as I quickly told them that the gala had been pushed to six thirty and the meeting was over. For some reason, I felt in that instant that my career in Nortel was over. It would take a full year to play out, and Clarence left even before I did, but I was not mistaken.

For my whole life, whatever the job, I wanted to excel, striving to be the best. But, before Nortel Networks, the longest I had ever stayed in one job was four years—as the business reference librarian at the University of North Carolina. Usually, I left jobs because I got bored, often relatively fast, as soon as my learning curve started to flatten out. I sought change naturally, not only changing jobs frequently, but also constantly trying to change the job itself. I was a change agent long before the term was coined. For me, change is about learning, growth, and development. After all, what's the alternative? Status quo? Backsliding? Boredom.

I never got bored in my seventeen years at Nortel. The environment didn't allow it. A dynamic company in a dynamic industry.

I changed jobs an average of every eighteen months. We some-times counted bosses per year instead of years per boss. My work ethic and my drive for excellence were valued and rewarded, often with more work. There was an unbridled spirit in the workforce at Nortel. Employees truly believed the mantra that we could be the number one telecommunications company in the world.

Then the dot.com bubble burst. And the telecoms bubble burst before we even realized it was a bubble. Nortel hit the wall hard, as if we didn't see it coming. Yet some of us did. Many had been warning for years that there were fundamental flaws in the demon-strated values of the company that would impede us from reaching our potential.

From the very start, in July of 1984, I had set about to change the company. I had only been with BNR (Bell Northern Research—the research and development subsidiary owned by Bell Canada and Northern Telecom) about three weeks when I came home and told my wife, "This is going to be a great ride. But it is not going to last. The company doesn't seem to value money; they piss it away." But the ride lasted much longer than I ever would have predicted. I joined at the entry level for a professional and rose to vice-pres-ident, a climb of six "bands," or one level of the hierarchy every three years. When I finally worked at the top level of the company, I took on my mission with a personal fervor. I was going to fix the company. I knew I had the insight to do it; I just needed the cour-age to develop the influence.

I slipped a few times, but I never wavered. In this book, I want to share a few of the stories that most impacted my learn-ing, some that added value to the company, some that may have missed the mark. My goal is twofold: 1) to provide some insight about how to drive fundamental culture change in large compa-nies; and 2) to present an argument that Nortel failed due to a flawed culture. The capability set that I grew is best categorized as "Organization Development." OD is a term with many defini-tions. It is a field with a mysterious, almost spiritual aura about it. The practitioners share some secret, you see; you either "get it" or you don't.

My definition of OD is highly influenced by Marvin Weisbord's *Productive Workplaces*[1]: if you want to get the most out of the workplace, trust the people who do the work to organize how to get it done. What a radical idea! And yet we don't get it. We continue to follow industrial age norms, driven by beliefs that you cannot trust the people. With size comes hierarchy. With hierarchy comes decisions that are further and further removed from the work. Those at the top of the hierarchy are more and more motivated to achieve short-term financial numbers. Out of that motivation, we have gotten Enron, Arthur Andersen, Tyco, Healthsource, ImClone, AOL/Time-Warner, WorldCom, AIG, Countrywide, the housing collapse, the bank bailout, the recession of 2008, and... the bankruptcy of Nortel.

Accounting developed as a science, but it has evolved into an art, driven by the Street's demand for quarterly earnings. Restatements have now become common. In fact, in the first quarter of 2004, Nortel had to restate its restatement! What this book will not do is attempt to assign blame to individuals. Many large companies tend to evolve blame cultures. When something goes wrong, it must be somebody's fault; someone has to be held accountable. And thus the fear!

Yet the reality is that mistakes are sometimes predictable. They happen because of misguided processes and flawed cultures, not always because of bad or incompetent people. In fact, despite a number of suits and court cases that are trying to find it, there has been no evidence of intentional wrongdoing at Nortel. Yet in 2001/2002, most shareholders lost over 90 percent of their accumulated wealth. How could this have happened?

Nor will this book attempt to describe the end-game, the final tragic decisions that led to bankruptcy and liquidation. For that story, read James Bagnall's *100 Days: The Rush to Judgment that*

---

1   When I mention both the name of a book and the author, with nothing else to add, I will not footnote it. Complete citations to all books mentioned will be in the Bibliography.

Killed Nortel. For many years, Jim covered Nortel for the *Ottawa Citizen* and I believe his analysis is spot on. Rather my thesis will be that the fear-based culture, and the leadership system that it engendered, created an environment that enabled poor decisions as inevitable.

I've structured my story into three parts: "Building Capability"— in which I describe my transition into Nortel and my growth as an OD professional in the context of Nortel's rapid successful response to the 1984 divestiture of AT+T; "Adding Value"—in which I describe those projects that most illustrate and define the culture and offers the possibility of what the company had to do to develop a sustainable culture; and, "Learning"—in which I reflect on what I learned about why the company failed and what others may be able to learn from it. The flow is thematic and is not meant to be a chronological narrative. I hope you can enjoy the ride—I sure did!

PART 1

BUILDING CAPABILITY

CHAPTER 1

WELCOME!

After accepting the offer to become BNR's technical librarian, for their new lab in Research Triangle Park (RTP), North Carolina, I gave the expected four weeks' notice to the University of North Carolina, where I had been the business reference librarian for four years. This upset Jim, the hiring manager at BNR, the R+D subsidiary of Northern Telecom. "What'd you mean you can't start for four weeks—I need you *now*!" I had applied for this job from an ad in a local newspaper, a full four months earlier. I had not heard from them, not even an acknowledgment, for three and half months. Then it was, "Can you interview in two days...and start in two weeks." No activity for three months, then near panic because he was late. I couldn't know at the time how prevalent this behavior would be.

I calmed Jim down by promising to work for him during the evenings, without pay. He sent me some library manufacturers' catalogs and asked me to order some equipment and start designing the space. Unfortunately, he had no answers for me when I asked about size and scope of the collection, and I wasted a number of hours sketching plans in a vacuum. I dropped them off in his office, but then didn't hear back from him.

I finished at Carolina on a Friday and took the weekend off—getting ready for the shift from public to private! The acceptance letter that I had received included instructions about where to show up for first day orientation, which would be held at the Northern

Telecom manufacturing plant in Research Triangle Park. I arrived about fifteen minutes early and parked in the "Customer/Visitor" lot, one of two times in seventeen years that I used this fancy entrance. The lobby was smaller than I expected: a receptionist behind a high counter, two or three chairs, and one sofa; but all pristine, clean, sparkling almost, and surrounded by dark cheery wood panels, lots of glass in the front, lots of light, and a couple of thriving plants.

There were a few other new hires. The receptionist made a phone call, and a woman from Human Resources came to escort us. We proceeded around the receptionist desk, up stairs that took us over the lobby, and into a classroom, well stocked with coffee, donuts, and juice. The room filled rather quickly as the young woman kept making round trips to the lobby, gathering the new arrivals, until we numbered close to fifty. There were barely enough chairs. Slated to start at eight o'clock, it was almost eight thirty before the woman from HR asked us all to take seats. "Good morning," she said. "Is there anybody here starting with BNR?" Looking around the room, I discovered only one other person had raised his hand. "OK, you two be sure to fill out BNR forms, not Northern Telecom forms…except for insurance and benefits, because you will be on the NTI plan for those."

This was followed by a succession of presenters from various HR specialties, none of whom seemed to know of any differences between BNR and Northern Telecom, and only a few of whom had a separate form for BNR. Midway through orientation, I realized that I was feeling inferior that I did not belong to the parent organization. The highlight of the day was a welcome and business overview, given by Alan Lutz, president of the local division, DSS (Digital Switching Systems, known locally as Switching). Alan was astute enough to ask if there was anyone from BNR, and then assured us that BNR was highly valued by "Northern." He also explained that Northern only owned 65 percent of BNR. The other 35 percent was owned by Bell Canada.

Then came the kicker. We were instructed to fill out one last form for our security badges and come up to the front of the room and have our pictures taken and we would be finished with orientation. I hurried through this form and was third in line to have my picture taken. When the photographer's assistant looked at my form, she said, in a sort of sad voice, "Oh, you're with BNR...Well, I have to hang a different color banner behind you, a purple one... Is there anyone else from BNR here?" Harold, an engineer, raised his hand from the back of the room, and I absolutely expected that since there were just two of us, she would ask Harold to come up, hang the purple banner, take our pictures, and then put the blue Northern banner back up. Instead, she said, "Ok, you two wait over here," pointing to the side of the studio area. For ninety minutes, we watched her take the forty-eight Northern Telecom new hires' pictures and only when she was one 100 percent sure that she was finished with them was she willing to spend the minute that it took to remove the four thumb tacks, take the two-by-two blue banner down, tack up the purple one, and take our pictures!

Then we had to get in the end of a line, as the lone HR person left in the room was using a company directory to look up the hiring managers' names, calling their admins, asking them to send someone to come get us, and "carry" us to the appropriate work area to meet our bosses. Were we going to ride on someone's back?

Thirty minutes later, about three thirty now, over two hours since the formal part of orientation had finished, I told her that I had been hired by Jim. About fifteen minutes later, a friendly, young woman came and asked for me. "Hi, I'm Ginny." As we were walking down the hallway from the classroom, she said, "You're going to like working for Bob!"

Stunned at first, but then sure I must have misunderstood her, I asked, "Who's Bob? I was hired by Jim."

The color went out of her face and her smile disappeared. She had guilt written all over her, as if she knew she had made a mistake and yet she was sorry for me at the same time. "Oh, didn't they tell you?"

"Tell me what?"

"I better let Bob tell you!"

Meandering through the maze of gray-paneled work cubicles, she took me to a "secretary's station." Yes, the people were called admins, but the workstation was called a secretary's station. Go figure. This was an open cubicle with a counter about four feet high. The admin sat behind the counter with her phone and computer, but could stand up and help whoever walked up without having anyone enter her workspace. I would learn later that many of them also used the furniture to effectively block anyone from going to see the boss without her permission. Ginny left me with Brisbane, who greeted me with, "Hi, I'm just a temp. Bob's on the phone. Wait here."

Bob's "office" was made out of ten-foot panels, which towered above the surrounding cubes, all made of six-foot panels. There was smoke wafting over the top of them, and I noticed that Brisbane had an air filter on the shelf in her station, trying to suck up some of the cloud before it got too far away. The flimsy door to his office was open, and I could see Bob on the phone. He was sitting behind his desk, balding head in one hand, telephone in the other, and a burning cigarette dangling from his lower lip. He took the butt out and flicked at an ashtray that was overflowing with butts and ashes, as he yelled at someone about delivery dates. Wearing a white shirt, collar open, no tie but a suede vest that would have looked appropriate on Clint Eastwood, Bob looked more like a construction supervisor than a business manager.

He hung up the phone roughly, angrily slamming it down. He stood up and started to pack his briefcase, as Brisbane went in and told him I was waiting. As she walked away, he signaled me into his office. He put his cigarette down long enough to shake my hand and say, "Welcome, have a seat." Without making any eye contact, he continued, "I only have a minute…have to catch the jet to Ottawa…leaves at four thirty."

Deeply anxious, desperately confused, absolutely nervous, I told him in a blunt statement, "I was hired by Jim."

"Oh," he said, without looking up, "We reorg'd last week. Didn't Jim call you?"

"No."

"Typical. Well, he was supposed to. But, look, I have to go to Ottawa. I'll be back in two weeks. Schedule some time, and we'll talk more then." He started to walk out, giving some last-minute instructions to Brisbane.

I interrupted and said, "What would you like me to do while you're gone?"

He stopped in his tracks, wheeled back into his office, put his briefcase down on the desk with a bang, but did not let go of the handle. He let out a heavy sigh, took a drag on his cigarette, raised his voice, literally yelling at me: "They told me you were a fucking professional...how the fuck am I supposed to know what you should do? Do I look like a fucking librarian? Don't *you* know what to do?"

"I am a professional," I yelled back, not as loud or as nasty as him, but, although defensively, loud enough to demonstrate I could stand on my own. He lowered his voice a few decibels and said, "Look, I have to go...figure out what to do and I'll see you in two weeks. Judy will help you!" I dared not ask who Judy was.

Bright and early on day two, I met Judy, who was Bob's "EA" (executive assistant). She and I hit it off right away. She had a great sense of humor and told me not to worry about Bob's hostile attitude, that he was really a nice guy. "Your priorities," she said, "are to get a work cube and meet some of the managers."

She sent me to the "Cabinet." Both BNR and Northern used that word to mean both the top leadership team and the office space they occupy. The term was derived from the physical offices, which contained lots of teak. I had to be sure to distinguish between business cabinets. At the time, the larger ones were for DMS 10 and DMS 100. (Digital Multiplexing Systems, the large telephone connection boxes, were rapidly becoming the cash cows of the company.) Most of the cabinet members were in a closed-door meeting, including BNR's lab director. I did, however, get to meet a number of their admins and I came away with a set of org charts, listing the power structures of BNR and the Switching division of Northern.

When I got back to Bob's area, Judy was happy to announce that she had acquired a cube for me. She led me through the rat's maze for several hundred yards, into an area marked by a small sign that said, "Technical Documentation." Noticing me glance at the sign, Judy said, "This is Tony's area…he runs Documentation. Don't worry; this is only temporary." She led me into a cubicle that couldn't have been more than ten square feet and told me to put together a list of office supplies and give it to Brisbane. While I stared at the empty desk drawer, realizing that there were no pencils or paper to put together my office supply list, Judy and Tony proceeded to have an animated conversation, not twenty feet from where I was, outside Tony's office, which was another one of those ten-foot high jobs.

"Judy, you've stabbed me in the back; now you are twisting the knife!"

"Tony, it's just temporary until I find something else!" I leaned out to stare at them. They saw me watching and listening and cut short their argument. Judy came by to remind me not to worry. "Tony's really a good guy. We argue all the time."

Tony was around forty, well groomed, starched white shirt and striped tie, trim mustache, and an accent that made me guess he was from India. He waited until Judy left before coming over to shake my hand. "Hi, I'm Tony. I own this area. That was nothing personal," he said as he nodded his head back toward his office. "It has nothing to do with you, really. I'm just tired of being victimized by Judy taking advantage of Bob's role as space planner. My group is growing, and I need to preserve my space for my own team."

"OK," I said quietly, "I feel so much better now; I really feel welcome here," sarcasm dripping from my voice. Tony was respectful enough not to disclaim. He just smiled softly and went back to his office. I hunkered down, arched my back, and picked up my phone. No dial tone. I didn't care. Who could I have called, anyway? My old boss at Carolina, Diane? "Can I come back? *Please?*"

I was about the thirty-fifth person hired in the lab and about a quarter or so of the population were managers, so I put a plan together to interview all of them. I started with Rod, the lab director. He told me to be sure to also interview the Northern managers that interface with the product developers, and he circled their boxes on my org chart. By the time Bob had returned, I had interviewed all the appropriate managers, crafted a vision as to what the scope of the library needed to be, and presented it to him. "Go for it," he said.

Two weeks later, Judy came by to see me with a big smile on her face. "I've got you another office!" She was so happy. She took me by the hand and led me through the maze, down the stairs, and out the door to a mobile home-sized, prefabricated office, which had a desk at each end. Clearly I was crestfallen, so Judy said, "Don't worry; it's just for a little while until we move." I met the manager who occupied the other end of the trailer. A Puerto Rican who had lived in New York, he was straightforward and friendly. Whew.

By this time, I had established an early view of a budget and was busy ordering books, documents, and journals, but not yet shelving because they wanted to wait until we moved before setting up a physical library. I was able to keep myself busy, though I had a disinterested boss, no real client expectations, and no friends. I plowed ahead, started a collection, and kept in touch weekly with the five or six managers who demonstrated some interest. I learned how to use COCOS (Corporate Communications System), a proprietary, early e-mail system.

One day, I began to notice an odor. I don't have a keen sense of smell, having been plagued with chronically swollen sinuses. In fact, I often miss smells that my wife or others pick up, so I knew that if I smelled something, it had to be strong. As my neighbor traveled most of the time, I was usually alone in the trailer. I called Judy and she came out to visit. "I don't smell anything." But she got a can of air freshener from facilities and sprayed it around to humor me.

It seemed to get worse day by day. The next time Judy came, she brought me some of those odor eaters that people dangle from the rearview mirrors of their cars. By the next week, she smelled it, realizing that it was not my imagination. She promised to get Bob to do something about it.

Soon, I was making daily calls to Judy and finally to Bob himself. He reluctantly took the time to spend five minutes to come and see me. At first denying that he smelt anything, he then turned on me and questioned my manhood. "Are you a fucking pussy, or what?" He was yelling at me again. "We have a business to run. We'll be moving to new space in another month or two. Would you please just focus on your job and stop bothering me?"

By this time, the smell was rank, dark, overpowering, a force unto itself. I had smelled skunk before, when my dog had gotten sprayed while I was camping. This smell, while different, carried the same impact. It started to make my eyes tear and my head ache.

I picked up the Northern Telecom directory and studied the services section. I called the head of facilities. He asked me to stop by his office and fill out an employee complaint. Fortunately, that brought immediate and sympathetic reaction. He came the next day and gagged when he entered my trailer. By early afternoon, he had a staff member crawling under the trailer, in the eighteen-inch crawl space. As the maintenance guy came out from under the trailer, he stood up next to me, but then abruptly turned away and dry-heaved. He turned back and said, "S'cuse me. Yawl got rats under your trailer. Dead uns. A few of em. I need to git some gloves and a trash bag and I'll haul em outtachere fer ye." Facilities had put poison out to combat a rat problem and the rodents had chosen my trailer as their final resting place.

I went home so they could remove the rats and fumigate the trailer. I was not supposed to come back to the trailer for a few days. Next morning, I went into Bob's office area. He was livid: "You went over my head!"

"I guess."

"You never fucking go to Northern with a BNR problem. We take care of our own problems."

"Well, you didn't take care of this one!"

"Don't you ever fucking go around me again, you fucking pussy librarian."

I bummed some space off my old pal Tony for a few days. I checked in with the Northern facilities director to thank him. "Why did you wait till it got so bad before calling?" he wanted to know.

"I called Bob," I told him truthfully, while knowing I was probably stepping right back into it.

"Oh, that explains it," he laughed. "Bob's typical BNR, but he forgets that he's living on my real estate. I'm glad you stopped by to explain that…I had thought you must be some kind of an idiot!"

"Well, you know what? Maybe I am."

CHAPTER 2

YOU CAN'T GET THERE FROM HERE

Four months after my start, Rod called and asked me to drop by his office. After some initial casual chat about how things were going, he said, "Well, basically, we think you're doing a great job with the IRC (Information Resource Centre), and I'd like you to set up a training department."

"But I don't know anything about training!"

"Good," he said with just the trace of a smile on his face, "you have a lot to learn!"

The immediate need was for technical training, specifically the tools and skills that a product designer (known as an MSS, Member of the Scientific Staff) needs in order to become proficient. With a few phone calls to Ottawa, I learned that corporate offered a three-week program designed by professional trainers, but delivered by experts from the MSS community. I talked to one of the designers and invited her to RTP. She helped me understand how to go about the process of getting a "volunteer" instructor from the lab, even to the point of giving me some lead names.

She also pledged support to help me carry off the first RTP iteration of the course.

The design and process were quite impressive: "Get the experts of today to teach the experts of tomorrow." The value exchange for the instructor was recognition, an opportunity to teach and to a certain extent a brief respite from the daily grind of "grunt" work. Although this was always negotiated with the instructor's manager, it was hard to honor—customer needs and product schedules could not be put on hold.

My first instructor had transferred from Ottawa, where he had once delivered the course. The Ottawa training staff was generous with both their time and their expertise, and the resulting feedback from both the students and their managers was quite positive. I considered the course a success, and said so in my monthly activity report.

Then I inadvertently stepped into a political minefield. I sent an e-mail to lab management, copying the Ottawa training staff, on some ideas that I had about how to improve the course. Twenty-four hours later, on a Friday afternoon, I received an e-mail from the technical training manager, under the subject heading, "Professional Concern." Its opening paragraph pierced my psyche: "Tim, I am appalled at the sequence of unprofessional behaviors that you have demonstrated. You have created a situation detrimental to development team productivity at RTP. For your records, here are separate instances for which I have witnesses and evidence of your unprofessional conduct. I send this to you in the hope that you will see what has happened and to act to correct." It went on to accuse me of undermining my boss by bad mouthing him in front of Ottawa staff, failing to adequately support the training program, and taking credit for work done by the Ottawa trainers. I was lectured about trust and cooperation. My suggestions were deemed "laughable in their absolute ignorance about the way training is developed and managed. There is not one perception that you offered that is new." Finally, it offered me some great advice about change: "In this organization, any-body but a slow learner discovers in a few months that if you really want to effect change in any program, you work supportively with the person responsible." But, I was threatened that my "unprofes-sional conduct" jeopardized the tremendous help and support I had received.

I was stunned, hurt, and angry. No one had been copied, so I immediately forwarded the e-mail to Bob and Rod. The next morning, a Saturday, I took the bait and sent an emotional, defen-sive reply, jumping right into the politicization of the issue: "My responsibility is, has been, and will be until my manager tells me otherwise, first and foremost to the region. I leave it to my man-ager—and the managers in the departments I serve—to decide the worth of my ideas and activities."

I forwarded my reply to the senior managers that I had held the training for. The few who responded indicated that a) my note was too strong and political, and, b) the training went fine. Mostly, they wanted to know when I would organize the course again. The only response I got from Bob, when I asked him about it, was, "Fuck Ottawa."

Rod also held his comment until he could look me in the eye. "You've been labeled a 'shit disturber'!"

"Is that a good thing, or a bad thing?"

He laughed. "Mostly good, but it will slow you down. Get up to Ottawa and mend the fence. You need to consider the functional heads in Ottawa as your dotted-line bosses. But, always remember, your straight-line bosses are here."

To succeed in this job, I learned that I would have to travel a lot. I don't know whether it was through nature or nurture, but I had inherited my mother's terror of flying. Before Nortel, I was a classic white-knuckler, prepping myself with Bloody Marys on the few occasions that I had flown.

The Eastern Airlines flight from Raleigh-Durham to New York was uneventful, arriving right on time at noon. I had an hour to get to my next flight. On a locator map, it was easy to find the national brands: Continental, Pan Am, United. Less obvious were the dozens of smaller airlines. I finally found Pilgrim: they had one gate tucked in the back of an obscure terminal. Nervous about connection time, I was anxious while the shuttle bus traversed a loop around JFK. To add to my anxiety, snowflakes began to flutter and the breeze picked up. I found the gate about thirty minutes before departure, heaving a sigh of relief. Little did I know.

I had taken the advice to bring only carry-on luggage. I was feeling smug; hoping to grab a drink after getting my boarding pass, but the gate agent burst that bubble when I asked for my seat assignment. She smiled sweetly as she said, "No reserved seats on this flight. First come, first served. And, oh, the flight is delayed. We don't have any 'equipment' yet." Seeing the consternation on my face, she was nice enough to translate, "We're not sure we have a plane." That was comforting.

Another passenger waiting for this flight tapped me on the arm. "Unfortunately, this happens all the time with Pilgrim. You should just settle into a good book." I hadn't brought one, so I bought a *New York Times*. Read all the news that's fit to print and did fine through the first hour. I walked up to the gate only to be advised, gently and kindly, that they were still working on "locating equipment." I bought a beer, picked up a *Daily News*, and breezed through it—lingering much more than I ever had over the sports pages, nurturing my brew. Upon finishing my second paper, I paced for a while, until the gate agent announced, "It looks like we have located equipment. We will be posting a departure time shortly." A small cheer went up from the handful of waiting passengers. True to her word, she did post a departure time, but not until a half-hour later, for a departure another sixty minutes after that.

Although I was growing quite hungry, my itinerary said that I would get lunch on this flight, so I did not want to fill up in the airport, even though it was now close to four o'clock. The departure time approached and slipped away and finally, about five fifteen, we began to board. There was no Jetway and we walked through a veritable blizzard to get to the plane. My fellow passengers, who had obviously been through this before, wearily shook their heads at me, as we climbed the stairs into the plane. Upon entering the plane, I stopped in my tracks. The plane looked like a retired World War II bomber that had been minimally retrofitted for commercial travel. The seats were bolted to the floor with no accoutrements like carpeting to distract the eye. No comforting panels on the sides of the plane, but rather bare and stark sheets of metal. The frame was naked, mottled with dark brown spots... was that rust?

"Take any seat," the attendant encouraged. There was an overhead shelf, similar to one on a bus, with netting on the side, where we stowed our carry-ons. We were not encouraged to place anything under the seats, which were also old, stained, even torn in a few cases. I found one that was not bleeding stuffing. The seatbelts, at least, seemed new and functional.

Snow began accumulating on the wings. The engines started, and the propellers spun into a blur. The lack of any extra panels or insulation caused the roar to be considerably louder than any other plane I had flown on. Any conversations on this plane would have to be shouted above the din. We backed away from the gate about ten feet, and then stopped.

The male flight attendant tried to shout above the noise. "Can I have your attention, eh? There will be a slight delay while we wait for the de-icing procedure." Then he disappeared into the cockpit. After about twenty minutes the engines shut down, the propellers slowly coming to a halt. I was looking around me in a state of near panic, yet others seemed to be taking things in stride, reading their books and newspapers. After about fifteen minutes, I couldn't take it, and I got out of my seat and went up and knocked on the tin cockpit door. The attendant opened it and asked, "Can I help you?"

"Are we taking off soon, or...?"

"Sir, we are trying to find a deicer."

"What do you mean, 'find' one?"

"Well, we only have the one gate here, so we don't own one, and we have to borrow one from another airline, and, naturally they are giving priority to their own planes, so it will take a while, eh."

It was almost another hour before a tanker drove up and started spraying the wings and the fuselage. Once again, the passengers cheered. We checked our seat belts as the pilot restarted the engines. Then we waited: five, ten minutes. The snow began to accumulate a little. Finally, we pulled out to the runway, and the attendant made a last check of the plane. "How long is the deicing good for?" I asked.

"About twenty minutes," he said.

According to my watch, it had been just over fifteen. "But..."

He cut me off. "Sir, would you please just sit back and relax." When we finally took off, it was about five minutes over the timeline, and I just held my breath, closed my eyes, and prayed. The plane rattled and shook, but got up above the clouds without falling apart. The attendant passed through with Styrofoam cups of water. Smiling, trying to get back in his good graces, I asked, "What's for lunch?"

He laughed right at me. "Lunch? It's seven o'clock in the evening!"

"I know, I know, but my itinerary says we get lunch, and I'm starving."

As I unfolded my sweaty and wrinkled travel plan, he leaned over to look at it. "Well," he said, "I know that we have purchased a few new planes and maybe you were supposed to get one of them on this flight, but I've been with Pilgrim for two years and I've never served a meal. Do you see a kitchen, eh?" He had a point, of course.

There was no galley. He had a very small cupboard on the outside of the cabin area that he was retrieving water and cups from. He seemed to be indicating that we should be thankful for the water.

When we landed, we deplaned and walked into the terminal building. We were directed through a Kafkian series of dark corridors, every now and then with a sign to customs, no other escape possible. Finally, after what felt like a half-mile march, we exited to a large room, which was filled with a number of lengthy lines, fifteen to twenty people in each. Clearly, we were to get on the back of the queue. The majority of the other arrivals were foreign. Lots of turbans and cameras but very little English being spoken. Thirty minutes of a slow shuffle step and it was my turn to talk to the uniformed custom agent.

"Passport." He looked at my open wallet. "Did I ask for a driver's license?"

"I was told I didn't need a passport to enter Canada."

"Do you have a passport?"

"No, sir."

"No passport?"

"No, sir."

Heavy sigh. "What is your business in Canada?"

"I work for BNR and I'm going to a meeting."

"What kind of a meeting?"

"About training."

He snapped my license down, raised his eyebrows, and asked, in a completely different, now interested tone of voice, "You are coming up here to train whom, exactly?"

"No," I corrected him, "I'm not coming up here to provide training; I'm going to a training meeting."

"What is the difference?"

Obviously growing more anxious, I nervously explained, "Well, training is standing in front of a group of students and teaching and a training meeting is a bunch of trainers getting together to discuss issues."

"Are you trying to insult me?"

Beyond anxious and absolutely scared now, I humbled myself and grew as deferential as I dared. "No, sir, I'm just trying to answer your question."

His response was to stamp my customs form and send me to a back room where I was escorted into a stark, thirty-square-foot office with just a table and two chairs and the overhead-hanging lamp seen in so many police shows. I kept assuring myself that I would not be beaten.

Two agents came in, one of them wearing a gun at his waist. First, they quizzed me on the information on my driver's license. Convinced that I was probably who I said I was, they went on to who I worked for and asked to see my company badge. "How long have you worked for BNR?"

"Four months."

"What do you do?"

"I run a corporate library."

"Why are you going to a training meeting?"

"We are thinking of combining the two functions."

"Eh? Do you mean you are going to move training jobs from Canada to the US?"

"No, sir. We are just talking about how to train US employees in the US."

They then subjected me to a lecture about how important it was to protect Canadian jobs and how inappropriate it was for Americans to come to Canada to threaten those jobs. I assured them that I understood; that I was no threat. They released me after about thirty minutes of this back and forth. It had been snowing heavily, and I was thawing as I waited at the rental car counter. Fortunately, the directions that Bob had given me were clear. I found my way to the hotel and parked the car. It was now close to eleven o'clock at night. I had not eaten for the entire day and the hotel restaurant had just closed, but the host took pity and brought me soup and a sandwich. Called home, took a hot shower, and grabbed a few hours' sleep.

Six thirty in the morning, out to the parking lot, only to find a row of identical white Tauruses covered with snow. No idea which was mine. After a momentary temptation to collapse in tears, I remembered that the license plate number was on my key chain. The third plate I dusted was a match.

Finding the lab was easy, but the parking lot was huge. My feet were soaked as I entered the building and asked for directions to the meeting room. Up a flight of stairs from the lobby, happy to see familiar faces, I called out, "Rod." He was with Alan Lutz, the president of Switching who had presented at orientation, his dotted-line boss. Rod was kind enough to introduce me, but Alan just smiled impatiently. Since they were each pulling a piece of luggage, I asked, "What airline were you on?"

"Oh, we took the corporate jet," Rod said nonchalantly.

"*What?*" People around us stopped to see what the raised voice was about and Alan was clearly annoyed. They were three or four steps above me on the stairway, looking down at me.

"Didn't anyone ever tell you about the jet?"

"No," I said incredulously. My mind suddenly filled with the memory of my first encounter with Bob. Rod exacerbated the situation by adding, "There were several empty seats; you could have flown with us."

"How long does the jet take?"

"Ninety minutes."

"Ninety minutes? It took me twelve hours to get here...on Pilgrim Airlines," I added expecting them to understand the enormity of that reference. "You guys should do something about letting people know about the jet."

Rod, kind as always, said, "Good point."

Alan, in an aside to Rod, simply said, "We have to get to the Cabinet." They hurried off, leaving me flabbergasted, both at the situation and at the audacious way in which I had handled it, accosting the most senior executives in the lobby. It would not be held against me. Indeed, I think it helped me gain respect.

Obviously, the knowledge base that had brought the company to the level of success it was achieving resided in Ottawa. Most of the major development decisions were made there. The corporate staff felt that they had the responsibility for any decision-making within their functions. The training manager who challenged me was well intentioned and authentic in her criticism. And she was right. Not in all the details and not in all her judgments. But I'd been out of line, arrogant, and aggressive, and could have been much more collaborative. We were able to look each other in the eyes and share feelings. We were able to get beyond emotions and build a working relationship. My first e-mail exchange had laid the foundation for this interaction. Forwarding stuff around to clients and bosses allowed me to get other views. Upon reviewing the whole situation, I also realized that I was distracting them from their day jobs. The e-mail preemptive strikes allowed us to vent and without it we might have avoided the learning.

CHAPTER 3

MONEY'S FOR NOTHIN'

The corporate jet provided a convenient connection each Monday, from Ottawa to Raleigh-Durham (RDU) in the morning, returning to Ottawa that evening. There was a small fleet of corporate jets ferrying execs around. Theoretically, any employee could get on it if they knew whom to ask. Underlings had to take the risk that a higher-up could bump us, even at the last second, even at the airport. The reservation process was tightly guarded by a few of the executive admin assistants, most of whom leveraged their boss' position to create her own power curve. I befriended the top admin at the lab. She was sympathetic when she heard the story of my first trip to Ottawa. She helped me craft a communications process that would disseminate availability. I took full advantage of my first experience really changing a lab process. I managed to land a seat on the jet at least a dozen times within the first few years. I was never bumped, and on only two occasions was the plane full.

The jet wasn't the only symbol of exuberance. Beer bashes took place at the drop of a hat. Fourth of July, Oktoberfest, even green beer on St. Patrick's Day. Annual picnic, new product launch, new marketing campaign, new hires, new recruits, new moon. Let's drink. Kegs R Us.

After my first annual picnic, several employees were weaving all over the road as they left the state fairgrounds in Raleigh. Wondering what the exposure was if someone got killed on the way home, I asked the HR manager, and he told me flat out it was significant, that there had already been several precedents where companies lost millions of dollars from similar suits. "Then why do we keep doing it?" I asked. Apparently they thought that the risk was worth it. BNR beer bashes were part of the tradition. They had had one *every Friday afternoon* in Ottawa for as long as anyone could remember.

The beer bash was just the proverbial tip of the iceberg. What I considered to be frivolous spending was ingrained deep in the culture: catered food at every meeting; bagels and cream cheese in the morning, pizza for lunch, popcorn in the afternoon; regular trips to Ottawa for four-hour staff meetings; popular literature and magazines for the technical library; speed reading and other trendy training available for the asking.

In an earlier job, back in New York in the finance industry, I had a collector who worked for me who regularly logged overtime. Said he had better luck getting customers in the evening. As his manager, I pored over his phone records every month. I saw a lot of calls to a number in Michigan, his home state. I asked him about them and he denied that they were personal. Fool. One night, I picked up the phone and dialed the number and talked to his girlfriend. Then I hung up and fired him. Not for making the personal calls, but for lying about them.

Once I became a manager at BNR, I expected to perform similar policing functions, but I was mistaken. Personal calls were tolerated, if not ignored. Once, an employee offered to pay for a number of long distance calls he had made. Couldn't find a process to let him do so. Never saw the bill. Finance told me to thank him for the offer, but decline it.

Predictably, there was rampant expense account abuse. There was a software problem in the central office of a phone company in the Northwest. When a switch is down, the loss of dial tone is doubly damaging. Revenues are irretrievably lost and customers are irate. Some of the engineers were directed to go fix it. While out there, after getting the customer back in operation, they decided to stay the weekend and go skiing. One of them bought new ski boots. He expensed them, and when he got back, his boss signed off. It's not like he wasn't already getting paid a premium, plus overtime, plus differential, plus a bonus, plus beeper pay.

Beeper pay. Virtually anyone who wanted one could request a beeper. That brought an extra ten dollars a day, *just for wearing it.* For some, seven days a week. Even if it never went off. If it did go off for a legitimate business need, and you had to make a phone call or two to help resolve an issue, you also got at least four hours OT.

OT! Overtime was being paid to salaried employees, many of whom worked at odd schedules and many of whom liked to play. Hacky sack tournaments could go on in the cubicle hallways for hours, followed by a break of company-provided soft drinks or coffee, and maybe a walk around the fitness trail or a game of volleyball. Then they'd get some work done. They might even work well into the evening. And put in for overtime.

Beware authorities that try to intervene. The facilities manager, citing fire codes and safety regulations, tried to enforce a written and approved policy. All decorations were supposed to be approved by his office. This attempt at enforcement was triggered by flagrant abuse from a particular department that had an affinity for dinosaurs. The designers had been bringing in blow-up dinos, stuffed dinos, dino models, and dino posters. A few started building primitive dino dioramas around their cubes. Very creative, but stuff was hanging from cubes, spilling into walkways, and cluttering up office space. The final straw came when someone hung a pterodactyl from a ceiling panel, damaging it.

Facilities sent the offending department a memo, attaching a copy of the written policy. The employees laughed and ignored it. Facilities appealed to HR for help but the managers told him to lighten up. For his trouble, he was gifted, anonymously and after hours, with a large inflatable dino in his office.

Forced into extreme tactics, facilities swept the office one night, confiscating and destroying all the dinos. The employees went ballistic and the whole lab became consumed by the issue for weeks. Other departments brought in sympathy dinos or other decorations. Sarcastic and satirical memos circulated, overdramatizing the loss of freedom. Facilities and HR were both subject to ridicule. It became an all-out war. Facilities swept every night. New toys appeared almost daily. To the facilities staff, this was a serious safety issue and they were trying to maturely meet their responsibility. To the offending employees, it was a game.

The rules of the game, and the score, were posted and disseminated on GOSSIP, a proprietary online bulletin board. It had been developed surreptitiously on company time, using company software and hardware. The Information Systems department had even begun to support it. They wanted it brought out from the underground into the mainstream, arguing that management could use it for announcements and such. Legal argued for killing it. HR mediated, established some ground rules and policy statements, and helped institutionalize it.

GOSSIP did do some good, was used for announcements and enrollment, but very quickly abuse spread. Some enterprising employees auctioned off, or just offered for sale, personal items. Social events were planned publicly, decades before Facebook. Then it got worse: political campaigning took place, as did religious proselytizing. Then the intolerable finally happened: sexist and racist remarks started showing up. HR had to do a number of interventions. A few employees got warned and finally one even got suspended for something that had been posted. GOSSIP became inundated with the resulting uproar. "Freedom of speech was under attack," by none other than the HR department...these fascists would have to be overcome.

The issue was referred to Lab Council, another cultural icon. The folklore was that in Ottawa, Lab Council was a governance body, with authority that helped shape the environment for innovative excellence. It dealt with serious issues like choice of software languages for specific product lines, how to resolve growth issues, and intra-lab moves. An Ottawa transplant had approached Bob, also from Ottawa, and Bob asked me to be a member and help set one up in RTP.

The first meeting was all about cigarette smoking. This was 1984, the year, not the metaphor. This was North Carolina, a state in prime tobacco road country. Council itself had about 30 percent smokers, and we agreed that they should sit on one side of the meeting room and the nonsmokers on the other side. Smoking in other meetings, and in the lab in general became the issue. For months. We did a survey of the population, which found that the majority wanted to outlaw smoking completely. The militancy of the smokers, coupled with the fact that Bob was a chain smoker, won out. Elaborate policies were developed: segregation in meetings, smoke-free zones in certain common areas like the cafeteria, and individual decisions on designating private offices as no-smoking zones. Facilities bought fans and air purifiers for anyone who requested them. Still, smoking would remain a top issue of Lab Council for three more years, until Northern imposed a corporate decision to ban all smoking in all buildings globally.

Other "critical" Lab Council issues involved whether BNR employees could go to Northern Telecom social events. Typically, BNR would want its cake and eat it too. For example, after much discussion and hand wringing about whether to have a jointly sponsored Christmas party, it was decided that BNR could hold its own, just for BNR employees and families, but all BNR employees and families would also be welcome at the Northern Telecom Christmas party. Weren't we special?

BNR management was often derisive of Northern, critical of its slow decision-making and weak management. Design managers argued vigorously and righteously for independence in development projects. Northern should provide the funding, of course, but trust the experts to do the rest. Northern management, on the other hand, returned the derision, considering BNR managers as prima donnas, wasteful eggheads more interested in technology than customers.

The corporate colors, evidenced by the banner background-ing each employee's picture on his or her badge, were symbolic of the separation. When a BNR manager crossed over to Northern, he/she would either "become blue," or, hopefully, would continue to wear "purple underwear," that is, maintain their allegiance to BNR. Yet, when Northern employees were perceived to have some-thing of value, BNR wanted the benefits of being blue. Christmas party logic was also applied to annual picnics. BNR had its own, complete with competitive horseshoes, alcohol and giveaways. Yet BNR families were also welcome to attend Northern's, which were held at regional theme parks: Carrowinds, King's Dominion, or Busch Gardens.

Month after month, Bob would reassure me that this was a learning curve; that eventually the Council would resolve the "en-vironmental" issues involved with a start-up and get to the busi-ness issues. It never happened, at least not during my standard two-year tenure on Council. Lab Council voted to keep GOSSIP with oversight and regulation. Eventually, though, HR and legal got together and shut it down.

The word that I used most often to describe the culture was "entitlement." Most of our new-hires were highly educated, high-ly intelligent. Masters degrees and PhD's were common. Many of them, enticed with exorbitant salaries and significant benefits, had come to BNR straight from campus. Of course they wanted it all, why not? During the baby boomer generation, parents followed the advice of Dr. Benjamin Spock, and the experts started worrying about permissiveness, but Gen-Xers went way beyond that. These people absolutely felt that management owed them a happy work place, owed them the environment that they had come to enjoy on campus. Management reinforced this mentality. Beer bashes, beeper pay, OT, refrigerators, candy machines, free snacks, coffee stations, fancy computers, workstations, cell phones, pagers, and maybe even an occasional pair of ski boots. All reinforced the entitlement mentality.

None of this would have been a serious detriment if we had the foresight to also instill business principles and customer value ethics early on. We did not. The entitlement mentality was actually institutionalized before the expansion into the states. The whole fabric of BNR was based on entitlement. All of the staff policies, processes, procedures, and systems were about one thing: getting your project funded. There was an extensive, documented, rules-based bureaucracy that enabled BNR to apply for funding from sponsoring Northern product departments.

Massive amounts of work, mind share, time and effort were put into preparing and submitting these development agreements. The ultimate goal, unfortunately, was self-serving: managers wanted to grow their departments. They craved more and more funding. Job grades were, to a large extent, based on numbers, but not always the right numbers. Since all of the sales revenues and earnings were attributed to the product and market organizations, the way BNR managers were compensated was largely based on how many people they managed and the size of their budget. So for an ambitious manager, growth of his/her organization became the goal. Getting funding from Northern was the way to do it. The funding organization became the "customer."

This was sustainable during a time of unprecedented market growth leveraged with the historical success emanating from BNR's leadership in digital switching technology. To a certain degree, it was even justifiable. Not only had BNR made Northern the largest and most successful company in Canada, it had catapulted the entire telecommunications industry into the digital era. (For more on the upside of the company's history, be sure to read Larry Macdonald's *Nortel Networks: How Innovation and Vision Created a Network Giant.*)

Make no mistake; BNR was absolutely a fun, productive place to work. And even if it was completely different from anywhere else I had worked, public or private, it was probably typical of the high-tech world, then and now. Our environment was a talent attractor. HR took line managers and even engineers on the road to recruiting fairs. The grunts could sell the environment better than the staff. But these conditions rooted and became the prevailing culture, resulting in business myopia, masking our ability to predict the inevitable.

CHAPTER 4

"HR HAS NO INTEGRITY"

The Information Resource Centre and the Training Department were two separate corporate functions. But in the Regions, the geographic research and development centers like RTP[1], both functions usually reported to the same manager. It gradually became obvious to us that the employees on our staffs had complementary, if not overlapping, capabilities. The common denominator was learning. Both functions had as their mission to increase the capabilities of the client through knowledge transfer, one through information dissemination and one through various forms of training, everything from standup to videos to broadcast satellite. This confluence affected our thinking, especially when we looked at it from the point of view of the client[2].

Every librarian learns the importance of the Reference Interview. The goal of the interview is to ascertain from the starting point of the client's presenting question what it is that the client really needs. For example, the client might ask if you have a copy of the Statistical Abstract of the United States. You might just tell him where it is on the shelf. Or, you might peel the onion a few layers by asking some questions. If you find out that the client is

---

1 In addition to RTP, at the time the regions were Richardson, Texas; Ann Arbor, Michigan; Mountain View, California; Montreal and Toronto in Canada; and Maidenhead in England.

2 Early on, we decided not to refer to internal people who used our products and services as "customers," reserving that important term for the external companies who spent money on the company's products and services. We agreed to refer to the internal folks as "clients."

interested in crime statistics, you would then lead him to the FBI Uniform Reports on crime, which will do a much better job meeting his needs.

One of the capabilities that I had to drill into my training staff evolved from the reference interview. Too often, Training had been content to answer the presenting question. This behavior was rooted in the way the function was measured. Training managers were reporting the numbers of courses held and the number of employees attending each one. This was summarized as person-days-training; affectionately known in the profession as bums in seats. While somewhat useful to grow training budgets and departments, these numbers proved useless in measuring impact on business.

Line managers, meanwhile, were content with this approach, content with the Training department "taking orders." A line manager would call and say, "My staff needs training in team building." A happy trainer, knowing we had training in team building on the shelf, would be all too eager to schedule the course. The client organization went through the course and got their bums counted. The stats got reported and everyone was happy. On to the next order.

Rarely, if ever, did we check back to see if the client organization was now acting more like a team. Even more important, we never looked to see if they were getting better business results. We decided to grow the needs analysis capability by leveraging reference interview techniques, flatly refusing to offer training courses without a thorough understanding of the business or performance issue that brought the client to ask for training. This was much easier said than done. Way too often, training was being commanded by some well-meaning manager further up the hierarchy. We started following the threads, connecting at higher levels, trying to understand why the senior manager was ordering the training. On too many occasions, the answer was rote. "Well, I know I'm supposed to invest in people development so this sounded good."

Our system conditioned this behavior. The performance management process had templates that had to be filled out by managers, one for each employee. Development plans had to be articulated. Good managers developed their people. Unfortunately, for the most part, "development" was defined as "training."

Occasionally, a manager would get frustrated with our approach and lecture me on my job: "You're supposed to supply the training, not question my intent."

"I think I'm supposed to add value to the business, not just do what I'm told."

To complicate matters, Rod decided that I should be accountable for all of the lab's *investment* in training. He installed me as a gate to the outside training world. If employees wanted to take a course outside the company, they would have to fill out a form, which required my signature. We wanted to assure quality control and stop sending employees to certain vendors who were not adding value. We built a database by following up with employees upon their return, asking them to provide a brief critique of the course they took, what they got out of it and asking them if they would take another course from the same vendor. We were able to establish who the quality vendors were and who some of the mill shops were.

When we tried to block somebody from going, by presenting the employee and his or her manager with information from the database, they would often be grateful and would ask us to help identify an alternative way to achieve the performance improvement goal. Unfortunately, in some of the cases, the employee and/or manager became defensive, either personally insulted that we were questioning their judgment or just being elusive about what they were really trying to accomplish. Often, this was evidence of the training-as-perk syndrome. "Well, Joe has been working real hard lately, and I want to do something for him and he's never been to San Diego, so I am sending him on this training course as a reward."

"OK, put that on the request form and I'll ask Rod if this is how he wants to invest his training dollars." But I was not at all comfortable in this policing role, imposing my value set on a line manager, not believing that it should be my call as to whether or not something like this was approved.

In several of the Regions, we formalized the combination of these functions, creating the first Learning Resource Centers. Much of the value-add of the LRC came from the power of the network. Networking like functions into what today we call communities of practice was already an established custom before I joined the company. In fact, it was part of the "core" role at the time, always the responsibility of the function head in Ottawa to lead the networks. We invested a lot in building these networks, regularly traveling for face-to-face meetings, complete with fancy dinners and expensive wine.

Despite being labeled a shit disturber, I was recognized for my efforts in my second year: my staff and I were awarded with the BNR RTP Award for Excellent Service, which was followed by a personal, corporate Award of Excellence for me. BNR flew my wife and me to Ottawa for a gala weekend celebration, culminating in a wild party at the Westin Hotel. It was at this dinner that I first met John Roth.

The company rag, *Insight*, featured a half-page article, complete with a picture of my smiling face in front of the library, "LRC EMPHASIZES SERVICE: In just 16 months, Tim Dempsey expanded the Learning Resource Center from two drawers of videotapes to a facility that offers users more than 2,000 books, magazines and technical reports and that delivers more than 50 in-house courses in a year." I exploited the process that allowed me to tweak the article before it went to print, and I plugged my belief: "'At BNR, we emphasize the need to work with the customer and provide them with value,' says Dempsey. 'In our case, the customers are BNR employees.'" I was careful to thank my staff and to give credit where it was due, closing with, "Dempsey adds that the success of the LRC can also be attributed to the strong support it has received from upper management at RTP. 'They realized how very necessary our group was to the successful operation of the lab as a whole.'"

Shortly thereafter, I experienced my first big reorganization. A new vice-president was coming to RTP, above Rod. Accompanying him was a seasoned PhD who was going to have all the staff groups reporting to him, in effect, a chief administrative officer for the lab. Both gentlemen were relocating from Ottawa. The lab had grown and someone decided Rod was not capable of running the place he had built. The employee population was confused; it appeared that the lab director was being punished, or blocked, but no one could understand why.

I was now on a peer level with my ex-boss, along with the heads of HR, Legal, Purchasing, Real Estate, and Finance. Apparently, I was the only one who was happy about this. Most of the others were upset that they would no longer be reporting directly to the lab director. Staff groups often get criticized, rightly so in many cases, for being disconnected from the business. It was hard to understand how adding yet another layer of staff hierarchy was going to help improve this image.

It's natural for organizations to clump their staff groups together. Line folks, the people directly responsible for the products and services, tended to see all admin as busywork. It's the stuff they didn't have to pay too much attention to, unless they became managers, and then they had to be sure to follow the right processes to be successful and cover their asses so they didn't get sued. I never bought the concept of "servant," never considered my role as any less important than a line role. Yet, I noticed that many of my peers were comfortable in the supplicant role. They were in awe of the line and saw their role as doing what the line *wanted*, rather than what the *business needed*.

At the very first staff meeting in this new configuration, I treated Human Resources as comic relief. The line always made a game out of spoofing HR, so why not me? Kerry Bessey had just moved to RTP from San Francisco. I had been hearing her name for months. Bob had been assuring us that she was going to "fix" HR, make it more professional and business focused.

Upon arrival, Kerry made it clear that she was hired to set up a "US core" HR function. Due to similarities in language and culture, many of the Canadian managers who had relocated from Canada to the States did not bother to learn or respect the subtle distinctions of doing business in the United States. Using demographic statistics to measure discrimination, for example, was a shock to them. I had been able to get the senior lab management team to sit through a half day of training on legal risks, at the end of which one of them said, "You have so many laws here and you're so lawsuit happy, maybe we should have just stayed in Canada?"

"Maybe *you* should have," I shot back.

In the States, we had issues around the lack of women managers and the small numbers of minorities at all levels. All of the execs were Canadian. They did not seem to be paying attention to the importance of fairness in the use of overtime and beeper pay, not to mention promotions and other job appointments. Kerry was going to establish US policies and procedures. She reported into "core" in Ottawa, not into the local RTP lab. She would not be running day-to-day HR functions.

In order to ensure that Kerry did not lend any extra credence to RTP by virtue of being housed there, she set up her group in a different area of the building, far away from local admin groups. Unexpectedly, shortly after she arrived, after moving her family across the country, Ottawa decided that US core would not be needed after all. She was relegated to being head of HR for RTP, reporting to the new CAO. This did not make her happy.

She became less happy, I am sure, every Monday at staff meetings when she had to suffer through my slings and arrows. "HR has no integrity," I would accuse with only a flimsy anecdote for evidence. "HR abuses its power," I would offer the next week. "HR follows a different set of rules than they expect everyone else to."

Most of these accusations were based on some anecdote I had heard or experienced. HR did have a lot of power and did exercise it with political expediency. For example, compensation rules were molded to fit individual situations, and staff people in HR tended to escalate the scale quicker than other staff groups. When I challenged this, I was told how unique and value-added the HR competency was and how the market dictated the comp just as it did for all groups. "Right," I would say sarcastically, my body language clearly indicating I didn't buy it. "And the LRC doesn't add value to the line?"

Our boss didn't stay very long. He was a well-educated, well-intentioned exec. He had managed a small discretionary slush fund for primary research projects, the Capability Fund, and seemed much more comfortable with university relationships than with customer or supplier business relationships.

One day he announced that he was moving on, was leaving BNR. This was my first experience with the corporate secret code for exiting execs. An organization notice that says such-and-such has decided to "pursue career opportunities elsewhere" often meant, "We asked him to leave and he agreed to do so because we are going to pay him a big fat severance package; an offer that he can't refuse." HR, of course, developed the code, and shaped the packages. The appropriate HR exec always eased the way, listened well, and helped the departing exec out the door. In fairness, we treated people with dignity on the way out, enabling them to keep their heads high and smile all the way to the bank.

I felt it coming before I read the line at the bottom of the notice: Kerry was named the head of the admin groups. She would be my fourth boss in less than two years. When they had eliminated

US core, I knew that running RTP HR was not going to be a big enough job for her. I honestly believed that it might be the end of my career with this company. I had not been kind, had been arrogant in my judgment and ruthless in my sarcasm. Was I the only one who thought I was funny? I needed to find out right away.

I put the notice down and immediately went to Kerry's office. Her door was closed and, although she seemed busy, she was alone and not on the phone. I leveraged the lab's open door policy, bypassed her admin, gave the polite knock, and opened the door. She looked up, slightly irritated at the interruption. She put her pen down, looked me in the eye, and gave a sly, knowing twitch of a smile. "Oh, it's you," she said, only a little disdainfully.

"Hi, Boss," I offered. "Congratulations on your new role."

"Thanks," she said. "Sit down for a minute." Would firing me only take a minute?

I was uncharacteristically quiet. The ball was clearly in her court.

"Look," she began, "you have been critical of HR ever since I got here. You have a big mouth and you act like a big shot." She took a breath. I took a breath, not thinking there was anything I could say to rebut. She was right. "So," she continued, "why don't you come inside and help me fix it?"

She had caught me completely off guard, and I was taken aback. "Sure," I said, instead of asking for details.

"Good," she said. "Now go away," dismissing me with a backward wave of the hand. "I have to get this report to Ottawa."

She would serve as my mentor for the rest of my time at Nortel and, over time, we became friends. In private, she was very tough on me, gave me unadulterated feedback on the impact of my abrupt style on both staff and clients. But publicly, she drew me deeper and deeper into the function, naming me Manager of Human Resource Development, then Human Resources Services, and within three years of joining the function, I was promoted to Senior Manager for HR, managing the entire function for BNR RTP.

She provided me with a green field to experiment. In 1986, we pioneered four-way feedback, now omnipresent and called 360-degree feedback. We instituted mandatory management training. We merged the career development process with the performance management process into an annual cycle that included peer reviews on development needs. We instituted a crude and early employee satisfaction survey. We discovered that one of the biggest dis-satisfiers to the entitled population was the lack of stronger career development support. We created a position, hired a specialist, and established a "Career Management Center." We installed a new language around career development from the Novation's Career Stages model[3]. That move alone raised the employee satisfaction score from 55 to 71. The entire telecommunications industry was flourishing, and I was having a ball, as the company and the lab continued to grow like an overflowing Petri dish.

---

3 The Four Stages, based on research pioneered by former Harvard Business School professors Gene Dalton and Paul Thompson, makes clear what high performers actually do and the contribution they make. By identifying the ways or "stages" in which people contribute and understanding what high performance is in each stage, companies can gain high performance from employees who understand how and why to increase their personal impact. See more at: http://www.globalnovations.com/Four-Stages#sthash.a4usGTqN.dpuf

CHAPTER 5

RATE THIS!

Once a year, the leadership of the human resources network sponsored a ritual gathering, the annual HR conference. All of the executives, with a selected few of the rising stars, met in some fancy hotel. The agenda was a mix of policy and business issues, team-building, and learning, including some white space for socialization and networking. The first one that I was invited to was at the North Raleigh Hilton in January 1986. It started out on Super Bowl Sunday, a major faux pas. The significance was totally lost on the Canadian planners, while most of the folks from the States were resentful. Televisions were rushed in to the corners of the dining room, but only the diehards stayed with the game, as Chicago quickly blew out New England, 46–10.

The meeting was facilitated by a couple of Ottawa-based, internal OD experts who had completely different styles. Cliff was out there, close to the edge of what one might consider conventional. He delved deep into the nuances of peeling layers of psyche off individuals to expose the hidden collective conscience of the group. We examined the underlying issues that we perceived to be constraining the business, but mostly we worried about how we in HR were going to add more value. It was an attempt at group self-actualization.

Jenny Gonzalez, on the other hand, was all process and flip charts. We needed action plans, and she knew how to get them.

The depth of her dark eyes drew her audience into her sphere. Polar opposite in style from Cliff, she exuded trust. If he was there to entertain and engage, she was all about focus and results. She radiated confidence and the knowledge of the business to demand instant respect.

The food was good, the drinks were free, and we had some fun. But those of us who were junior managers were continually conscious that our behavior was being monitored, and we were being judged. How we performed in these offsites would be a data point that could be used to further, or impede, our careers when the execs sat down to discuss our development. Nonetheless, I spoke my mind, at least a few times in my highly judgmental attitude of superiority. At the end of the three days, although totally exhausted, I had little imagination that we had accomplished anything truly noteworthy. But I had expanded my sponsor network, as Jenny would become a second mentor to me.

On the third and last day of the conference, we heard that the space shuttle *Challenger* had exploded. Our issues were set in a new perspective, and they no longer seemed so vital. We applied the disaster as a metaphor, though, symbolizing the precarious nature of the engineering profession. The scientists in the room seemed to take the explosion personally, like it was a failure of all science. Particularly poignant for us, as for the rest of the world, was the loss of innocence with the death of Christa McAuliffe, the elementary school teacher, and the impact this event would have on kids everywhere.

The network met the next year for a full week in Mont Ste. Marie, a trendy ski resort outside Ottawa. Many of us were indignant that we had to travel on a Saturday, causing us to be away from our families for seven nights. Especially when we got there and had to suffer through the Est[1] guru. He attempted to hypnotize the whole group, at the same time. The HR manager from California succumbed and was snoring. Others had their eyes closed and seemed to be in a trance. It was all I could do to keep from laughing as I peeked out from under my lids to see who else was cheating.

That night, by the fire in the lodge, I started to strengthen my relationship with Kerry. We each had a few drinks and shared a few laughs. She took her business mask off, just for a moment, making it clear that she, too, valued balance and family above the work. The exec persona that she had to wear was only one of her selves.

We spent the next few days in structured programs. Cliff tried to teach us some neuro linguistic programming[2] so that we could better manipulate our clients. I began to make better use of the white space, became less concerned that I was being observed, and became more comfortable that I belonged in this group. I was a sponge for the learning, consciously aware that I was growing, that I was interacting with corporate execs, PhDs, writers and teachers from Harvard; and I was holding my own. My self-confidence grew dialogue-by-dialogue, intervention-by-intervention.

Meanwhile, back home, I was occasionally stumbling as a manager. I wanted to be friends with my staff; I wanted to be liked. I got in the middle of, and tried to resolve, petty conflicts. The majority of HR employees were females. In the sexist parlance that we used at the time, there were a lot of catfights, and I got scratched a few times. I allowed personal problems to be aired in the office.

1 "Est"—in psychology, a treatment intended to help people toward psychological growth, in which they spend many hours in large groups, deprived of food and water and hectored by stewards. (TheFreeDictionary.com)

2 NLP, or neuro-linguistic programming, is a form of behavior modification used in the professional world as well as in parenting. NLP involves an in-depth understanding of mental, cognitive, and strategic thinking that are the processes behind how we behave. It is a very powerful skill for communicating. (NLPU.com)

I started to embrace the persona of a controlling patriarch. And I brought my Queens dirt-mouth with me. The first time I went through four-way feedback, I was surprised at the extent of the damage that my language was causing me. In New York, in the credit world, every third word began with the letter "F," which was used as a noun, a verb, an adjective, and an adverb. In the South, I was offensive, crude, sexist, and a sinner.

I had made a few hires of people who could not coalesce with my rudimentary style and I exerted the power of my position to let them go. I learned how to "pass the turkey," a common practice. Someone not working out? Give them a good recommendation, and let them go work somewhere else in the company. I gave feedback during performance reviews on how people were perceived by their peers.

Somehow, above all the soap opera diaries, we continued to excel as an organization. Northern Telecom began to notice. John Hofmeister, who had joined the company from General Electric, invited me to attend his weekly NT HR staff meetings. I was flattered, punctual, and attentive. I knew I was in the presence of a master. His ability to focus on the business, to examine and resolve issues, to get beyond the high school level politics that sometimes prevailed, enlightened me.

He invited me to an offsite at the Wye Plantation, on the Eastern Shore of Chesapeake Bay. We were supposed to be talking about how to improve communications in the function, but he had a hidden agenda as well. The company was going to have to tighten up. We were spending too much cash; our margins were deteriorating. Somebody finally got it! We were going to reduce costs, downsize the population, restructure the business, and we were going to start with HR. He asked me to be on a transition team, letting me know that within a few years, Northern would absorb BNR and stop operating it as a separate subsidiary. It was correctly perceived that BNR's independence fed the historical aloofness that allowed the R+D population to pursue technology innovation instead of customer value.

John was in RTP only briefly. He moved to Nashville to become head of HR for all of the United States. He brought in a few of his key OD staff from GE. He connected me to the HR Strategic Partnership at the University of Michigan. David Ulrich[3] and Noel Tichy[4] were the professors who had done a lot of the research on which Jack Welch based his leadership development program. Tichy was a key consultant in setting up GE's renowned Croton-on-Hudson leadership development center.

Ulrich was tracking the changing value-add of HR. His data showed that the most successful companies valued the business acumen and change management capabilities of their HR function. The old value-add of functional expertise had become business necessity. Sure, HR had to provide processes and tools for compensation, benefits, and labor relations. Furthermore, it had to perform these benchmark basics with effectiveness, cost, and otherwise. But this just kept the business open. Competitive advantage came from the new capabilities.

Kerry "crossed the street," replacing John as head of HR for the Raleigh area divisions of Northern Telecom. She stepped right into the center of what was increasingly referred to as the Switching Mafia. Before she left, she conducted my performance review. She gave me an "Achieved," the rating applied to 80 percent of the lab's population in a forced bell curve. She also gave me some tough feedback from the peer review, saying that she tried to present me as an "Exceeds," but had received push back from the executive management team. It was clear that my abrasive style and my arrogance, the very stuff that was so irritating to my staff, was definitely a detriment to my career, as my boss system was growing exasperated with how high maintenance I was.

She did her best to explain to me that while I accomplished a lot, my style was grating, with the resulting impact that my level of influence was compromised. It was her argument, clearly stated,

---

3 We used a number of Ulrich's books, especially *Human Resource Champions.*
4 We also used a number of Tichy's books, especially *The Transformational Leader.*

well-articulated, and in hindsight, spot-on, that I could get even more done if I would adapt my style to one that was more politically correct.

While standing in my office, she pointed to an icon of the problem: on my shelf was a coffee mug that someone had given me that said: "I'm OK; You're a Shithead!"

"Get rid of it! You cannot have vulgarity in your office. And what's with the tinted glasses?" I gestured up at the fluorescent lights. She continued to berate me. "You're in HR; people will never trust you if they cannot see your eyes."

I tried to defend myself. "Kerry, I only fight for the 'right' things, right for the business, right for the client. I'm not politically motivated. I'm not a power monger."

"Motivation is irrelevant when it comes to how you're being perceived. Don't you see that all of that is irrelevant if you are not being listened to?"

She refused to change the rating, the first one I had gotten below "Exceeds." I went apoplectic: "You're being unfair." She intended to humble me, but I was incensed. "What's the appeal process?" I wanted to know.

She was outraged. She backed me into a corner and said, "See, this is exactly the immature behavior that I'm talking about."

"Immature? HR has an appeals process in the policy guidelines that it issues to all employees, but if I want to use it, I'm immature? This is exactly what I'm talking about, what is still broken about HR." She walked away in a huff.

I went to the compensation and benefits manager for counsel—mainly wanting to make sure that I understood my rights, rather than for his personal advice. He confirmed that I did have the right to appeal to Kerry's boss, Rod, and even to *his* boss if I insisted. He also advised me not to do so. "What do you expect to get out of it?"

"Well, obviously, my comp is affected by the rating." Guidelines suggested a significantly higher percentage of annual merit increase for an "Exceeds." He proceeded to get out his notebook with all the comp of all the employees in the lab. He read my salary history, out loud, and suggested that it was his opinion that I had one of the most, if not *the* most, accelerated history of anyone in the lab. That is, for the time I had been there, I was paid a higher percentage above my starting salary than anyone else.

"I don't see the relevance," I shot back. "If I perform at a level above anyone else—if I am contributing at a level commensurate with my comp—why is this history relevant? And, furthermore," I droned on, "I resent the fact that you are trying to talk me out of using policy that was written to protect me...Do I not have the *right* to make this appeal?"

With a heavy sigh, he dropped the argument. "Of course you do; I was just trying to help you be clear what you want out of it."

"To be treated fairly."

He closed with a brief lecture that the right thing to do was to let Kerry know, not to surprise her. I took this as good advice, thanked him, and went to see Kerry. She was beside herself, not out of self-concern, but out of the absurdity of the situation. "Don't you see," she all but yelled, "this is exactly the type of stuff I'm talking about!" She walked away shaking her head.

I sent Rod an e-mail, copying Kerry, explaining the situation, my formal appeal, and requesting a meeting. Rod left me a voice mail, saying he would stop by my office the next day. Of course, he talked to Kerry first. When he came to see me, he closed the door, grabbed a chair, and put his feet up on my desk. We chitchatted for a few minutes before he took on a more serious tone. He announced at the outset: "I'm not going to overrule Kerry and change the rating. Let's be clear about that. Kerry likes you. She's trying to help you. You're a key resource and we all know it. Why don't you let Kerry help you be more productive?" I felt defeated and he could see it. He shook his head and laughed. "And lighten up a little," he said. "Don't have a heart attack...enjoy yourself."

I *was* humbled, embarrassed that I had taken his time away from the business to deal with my immaturity. I ended the conversation quickly, realizing that I had to pay attention to the feedback. It was irrelevant that I could prove that I had achieved my objectives, met my milestones. I began to see that it was just as important to my development as a leader to pay attention to *how* I achieved them.

We shook hands and I thanked him for his time. I immediately signed my form and brought it down to Kerry. She was kind; not bitter, not angry. She did ask me to sit down while she signed it, and then gave me the best advice I have ever gotten as a change agent. "Look," she said, "you can't fix everything that is wrong with the world, or even with BNR. You must choose the things you are going to fight for. First, you must decide if the issue you are angry about is really important. Will fixing it have positive impact, either on business results or on the customer? If not, drop it and work on something that will. Secondly, you must decide if you have the skill set to help improve the situation. And finally, if you decide it is important and that you do have some value to add and skills to help improve, face the hardest question. Will the environment allow you to succeed? Do you have the influence and the opportunity— can you really envision things changing? Or do you know from the outset—for whatever reasons—that a given situation is unlikely to change? Choose to work only on those things that you believe are important to the business, not just morally right in some arbitrary value system; that you have skills for, and that you actually can imagine changing—and then work on them flat out. Most important…stop trying to make *every* issue your own personal crusade. You are losing credibility and that is preventing you from succeeding on the really important ones!"

CHAPTER 6

GROWIN' UP

One day in the early '90s, Kerry called an impromptu meeting. She was so emotional I thought somebody must have died. "John is leaving the company." She could barely get the words out. Larry Bossidy, Hoffmeister's ex-client at GE, had accepted the CEO position at Allied-Signal and John was going to join him. Kerry was promoted to replace him and moved to Nashville.

Before she left, she informed me, "We're going to downsize HR, including BNR. You need to cut your staff from thirteen to six."

"What? How can we do that? I don't have anyone sitting around, you know?"

"Yeah, but you have some luxuries."

"Give me an example."

"The career management specialist is one example."

"She's single-handedly helped me raise the employee satisfaction twenty points."

"Too expensive. Look, NT is downsizing, too. If your people are good, help them get jobs over here."

We only had a few weeks for this exercise, and I put most of my energy into placing people, successfully landing jobs for all of my staff. Concurrently, I networked in high gear, asking Kerry and even John, who was nice enough to buy me dinner on his way out, "What about me?"

I was offered the luxury of a choice. I could stay at BNR and try to serve the growing entitled population, which now numbered close to a thousand—try to do the same work with half the people. Or, I could cross the street. Several of the HR execs encouraged me to take a position as Senior Manager[1] for Organization Development for the Raleigh area. I'd learned that it's wise to please your sponsors, so the decision was really a no-brainer.

I was going to be working for Jim, who also had responsibility for staffing and recruiting. I had met him at the Wye Plantation retreat. He was a relative new-hire, having been with the company for about a year. He was a seasoned professional, exceptional in that he had experience in other companies. Unfortunately, he had not been enrolled in the decision. When I went by his office, his door was closed, and he was on the phone; but I knocked, cracked it a bit, and whispered, "You got a minute."

He held his finger up, indicating I should wait, and then pointed to a chair. He finished up quickly and came out from behind his desk. "Hi," I said, "I understand that I'm going to be working for you?"

"Yeah," he mumbled, "I heard that, too."

"You don't seem to be too happy about it."

"I'm not. In fact, I'm pissed off."

I could feel the blood draining out of my body. What the heck did I do? What has he heard? "Look," he said after a painful pause. "It's not about you. I'm just not used to having other people do my hiring for me. But John and Kerry both say you're a good guy, and I understand it's a done deal, so I'll get over the anger. What exactly is your experience in OD anyway?"

"Uh, none I guess."

"What! Damn! Why did they do this to me?"

"Just lucky I guess."

---

1 Despite the fancy title, a "senior manager" was not an executive. It was actually the second level of management, the first to be a manager of managers. It was also the first bonus eligible layer. Called a "C level," at BNR, the new compensation scheme was the great equalizer. I was not being promoted. This was a lateral move, from one Band 8 position to another. I would report to the next level up, a Band 9, level B, known as a director.

"Look, I have to make a few calls. Come back and see me to-morrow morning and we'll figure out what we're going to do about this."

I went to see the OD professional that I would be replacing, who was also heading to Nashville with Kerry. He told me not to worry. "Jim's all right. He'll come around."

"But, I don't even know how to define 'OD,' and now I'm the senior manager in it?"

He proceeded to tell me of the different philosophies and schools. His master's in OD was from Brigham Young University. He had strong capability on the technical side: organization design, work processes, and business structures. Jim, on the other hand, had his master's in OD from American University, which was affiliated with National Training Labs (now known as NTL Institute). The NTL approach emphasized the soft side of OD, human interaction as the focus of all effectiveness. "Stop worrying. OD is all about logic and process. It's all about strong analytical skills. The way you practice HR *is* OD. It comes naturally to you. Forget about the label."

Jim made his phone calls, and his bosses convinced him that I was his guy. He encouraged me to go get some basic training, and I registered for the NTL course on Work Unit Reorganization. It was a three-day course in Washington, and like all NTL courses was very experiential. In fact, they referred to their courses as Human Interaction Labs. We learned what motivates people to work. The higher up the pay scale you go, the less pay acts as a motivator. Overlay Maslow's hierarchy of needs[2] and you discover that after

---

2 For an introduction to Abraham Maslow's model, see http://www.simplypsychology.org/maslow.html#needs5

people have enough pay to provide food and shelter, they start to focus on adding value and being valued.

We explored Marvin Weisbord's *Productive Workplaces*, which would become my bible. Weisbord was a journalism major who had become an operational expert, running his own factory. HR consultants were always telling him he needed OD help, so he decided to learn for himself what that meant. He surveyed the literature and summarized the results in his book, basically simplifying the field to a fundamental belief: If you want to organize the work so that it is most productive, trust the people who do the work to organize it for you. His approach revolutionized the role of management, away from the Taylor theory of scientific management[3], which said that people cannot be trusted, must be carefully directed and controlled. Weisbord believed that management should shape an environment, a culture, in which people can achieve their own potential. If the employees are motivated and developing, if they are adding value and being valued, they will be the most productive.

The facilitators were flexible to changing conditions, reacting, and adapting as the lab progressed. In the middle of the second day, an "intervention" was needed. A couple of loading dock supervisors from a brewing company in Texas had managed to offend a senior executive from the World Bank, who happened to be from Ghana. She publicly accused them of racism. The instructors instantly adapted to the situation. They halted the course and broke us up into small groups. We examined the issue of racism in the workplace until late in the evening. They stayed on it until the World Bank exec felt the issue had been adequately addressed, until she gave them "permission" to move on.

"This is what OD is about," they explained, "doing whatever the people in the room need you to do to be more effective." I was hooked.

---

3 Frederick Winslow Taylor, *The Principles of Scientific Management*, 1909.

I started to examine and sort out the responsibilities of the role I had accepted. One was to "approve" organization notices. There was a stack of them backed up. Reading through them, I could not figure out how to add value. I called a few of the issuing managers, and asked them questions about their intentions, but mostly they were annoyed at the intrusion. "Just sign the damn thing so that I can issue it," was their general attitude.

"No," I said.

This went over big and by the end of the day, Jim was in my office. "What's going on with the org notices?"

I waved the stack at him. "They're all done. They don't want any help. They just want my signature, and I can't for the life of me figure out how my signature is going to add value. I might be able to help if they call me before they decide what they want, but I'm not going to sign just because somebody expects me to. I'm not adding value, and there is no opportunity for me to add value. Let them sign their own damn org notices."

He picked up the stack and left, turning back to say, "Cool. I like you."

Shortly thereafter, another HR reorganization: Neal, a line executive who agreed to a "staff" assignment as a development move, became head of HR for the RTP region, and I would report directly to him. At his first staff meeting, Neal used a conversational tone to present his perspective to his new staff. "Let me tell you what the line thinks of HR," he began, with a big smile on his face. "We know that we have to fool you. We know you have lots of power; that the top execs listen to you when it comes time to recommend leadership promotions. We know that you can impact our careers, one way or the other. Some of us are disdainful about this, and avoid you, to avoid having you see our disrespect. Others, though, the more clever ones I think, embrace you. We drop in your office and chat. We ask your advice. We pretend to listen. We thank you. We take this time to fool you, to trick you into thinking that we respect you. Meanwhile, we are laughing at ourselves for playing the game. This game is a diversion from the terror of the marketplace. It is comic relief from running the business. And it works. You recommend those of us who treat you this way. You block the others by talking about their management styles as abrasive or business immature. Most of you have never run a business and don't have a clue as to what we're going through."

He paused for dramatic effect and looked around the table. Most of his direct reports were looking at their feet. "I want to change all that. I want people to respect you because you can help them with their businesses, not because you have all this power you can yield."

After the meeting, I quickly discovered that I was the only one who was impressed. I was delighted, both at his message and at the straightforward, authentic way in which he delivered it. Most of my colleagues from Northern were career HR execs, many of them holdovers from the days of personnel management. "This guy's a jerk," they said. "We have to get rid of him."

A large part of this job was "rolling out" corporate programs, an opportunity for transitional learning. I had gone from being a relatively big fish in a small pond to a minnow lost in an ocean. After a few years with decision-making authority over my function, I had to learn the art of teamwork. Universities have committees, but corporations have teams. Project teams, tiger teams, cross-functional teams, development teams, and leadership teams. In fact, working together, we accomplished a lot. We revamped the performance management process, leveraging some of the learning we had about the importance of personal growth and strengthening the business in addition to meeting individual milestones.

We supported the creation of and facilitated the meetings of the Raleigh Leadership Council (RLC). We encouraged all the executives in the geography to get together and talk about shaping the culture. The RLC instituted 360-degree feedback across the entire management team. We did research for and helped design a major restructuring. The executives were beginning to understand that the product and technology driven approach that had made them successful might not be the same approach to sustain that success. Indeed, the driving force of the business needed to come from the front end, from the market, from the customer. We used strategic alignment[4] models to leverage organization changes: *implementing* and *executing* strategy were clearly more important than *developing* strategy, yet much more time was put into developing.

Not all efforts were successful. We strove to develop a meaningful Key Resource Development (KRD) program. Leadership wanted to identify the top 5 percent of the company. We established criteria, definitions and a process for identifying and rolling up the names. Managers spent hours and hours making and refining lists. Paul Stern, the CEO during this period, wanted to have a book of pictures that he could carry around so that he would know a KRD if he happened to randomly bump into one. So we hired a photographer and took portraits. Although flattered to be in the book, I became frustrated at the bureaucracy. All the effort went into producing the list and getting the pictures. There was no time or energy left for *doing anything* with the lists. That is, having a list became the objective, not developing the people whose names appeared on the list.

---

4 We brought in Norm Smallwood, from Novations. You can read about the approach to "Strategic Improvising" in *Real Time Strategy*.

As I increased the span of my network, opportunities arose for more specific local projects. I began to master group process facilitation skills, leveraging tools that I adapted from a range of vendors. Inspired by Weisbord, we designed and delivered Future Search Conferences, getting "whole systems"[5] in a room, enabling large groups to redefine their own purpose, craft their own vision and develop their own strategy.

I matured as a manager, getting to know and becoming much more comfortable with, deeper layers of myself. I had been recommending the Center for Creative Leadership's (CCL) Leadership Development Program[6] for a number of years. Most who took it came back raving about how it changed them, helped them develop as a leader. Only once did someone come back and say, "I knew all that stuff about myself, but I don't want to change." Too bad for him. He was "down banded" a few years later and a few years after that was asked to leave.

If self-awareness is necessary for learning, assessment is necessary for self-awareness. It was time for me to experience what I had been recommending. The program costs several thousand dollars and demands a week away from the workplace. It was a measure of Nortel's commitment to learning that it was willing to sponsor these types of programs. The preparation guidelines suggested that I needed to set aside at least eight hours to fill out all the assessment tools. I left it till the last night, figuring I could knock it out quickly. I was up until four in the morning.

---

5 There are a lot of definitions of "whole systems," a key concept in OD work. For the purpose of Future Search, Weisbord, defined it as "the broadest temporary planning community feasible for the task at hand. That means maximum variety and diversity of interdependent people." *Discovering Common Ground*, p. 66.

6 For a complete description, see http://www.ccl.org/leadership/programs/ ldpoverview.aspx?v=1.1

I took the course in San Diego, one of the CCL proprietary sites, which included a partnership with Outward Bound. Toward the end of the week, participants get feedback from a trained psychologist who has been observing them. Mine told me, "You have real issues with trust. Most people trust others until that trust is betrayed. You, on the other hand, don't trust anybody until they prove that they deserve it."

"Uh, isn't that how the world works?"

"Well, research suggests that it works that way for about 25 percent of the people. You're in that minority." I blamed it on growing up in New York City, but she wouldn't let me off that easily.

At the graduation ceremony, people share their feelings. Several cried, especially after we listened to Harry Chapin's "Cat's in the Cradle," the folk-rock staple of lost opportunity. Too many of us were leading "unbalanced" lives, focusing on work to the detriment of family and community. We all designed and shared our "action plans." I had glimpsed some layers of myself that had been hidden.

Within the next two years, I was promoted twice, first to generalist director in HR. Generalists are the folks who provide the advice and counsel, the hand holding, high touch service that keeps the work flowing. As the name implies, a generalist knows something about all aspects of HR, but is not necessarily a specialist in any of them. Duties include everything from staffing plans to layoff events. As a director, I was the liaison to the business cabinet. A team of generalists who reported to me supported the employees who reported into the cabinet level clients. Assigned to the Marketing Operations group, I was in the thick of internal politics. Reorganizations and promotions occurred continuously.

Marketing Ops was responsible for pricing; including negotiating long term deals in collaboration with Sales. My client, the vice-president, could expect a monthly call from product presidents, if not the CEO, to cut deals, discounts, and such, to assure that the division would make its numbers. He could authorize special sales incentives and seemed to pull off the impossible, month after month. Back in a hard-walled office, this time in a business cabinet, I was in close proximity to my clients. I felt the daily stress that propels the work ethic. My normal day was seven to seven. Many days I'd get home at ten or eleven, after my kids were asleep. Work vacillated between managing and coaching my staff to working the unforeseen issues that arose to surprise us every day. I learned that the art of coaching executives had much more to do with the ability to listen than it did with the need to give advice.

As soon as I grew comfortable with the generalist role and really learned my client's business, I was promoted to assistant vice-president of HR for Global Customer Services. I had never met this client, Eric, but I was aware of his reputation and remembered that he had been a winner of the Spirit of Northern Telecom award, the highest corporate recognition that can go to an individual. He was based in Dallas and had direct reports all over the globe. Eric was very clear in his values and his beliefs. We had one conversation, over the phone, and we hit it off. Without hesitation, I accepted the promotion into the role.

Global Customer Services seemed to be an idea whose time had come. When Paul Stern took over as CEO, he referred to the various businesses as "warring tribes," and many of the customers were victimized by our internal skirmishes. One executive characterized our image, as seen by our customers: "How deep does whale shit sink in the deepest part of the ocean? That's where you'll find our reputation."

Too many of our functions had allegiance to the organization to which they belonged, rather than to the mission of their function. For example, each business had its own customer service organization. Just as local sales departments would try to push their own products, local customer service departments would try to fix/service their own products. The dilemma, of course, was that very few of our products were stand-alone. Our value proposition was in the interworking of our products, in the networks we built. This issue had come out too clearly in customer satisfaction surveys: when a network went down, we needed multiple units to fix it, with coordination sloppy at best. The mission of Global Customer Services was to consolidate all customer services into one organization, to assure that we provided one face to the customer, and resolved internal disputes off premises.

Eric wanted to have his first staff meeting in Raleigh, to take on the so-called "Switching Mafia," the long-tenured managers from the division that had for many years represented the cash cow, and therefore the power base, of the company. We started with a dinner meeting: pizza and salad in a conference room.

The RTP regional customer service vice-president was on my case the whole night. I was first on the agenda, to present a view of what the organization development approach was going to be: we were going to focus on mission and vision first, then strategy, organization design, and staffing. He continuously interrupted me, challenged me, and seemed to be actively baiting me, always with a sly smile on his face. The meeting ended shortly before midnight, and I cornered him before he could get out of the room. "What was that all about?" I asked directly.

"We always like to break in a new HR guy by giving him a hard time...it's a kind of a sport. Most HR guys don't understand the business and can't take the heat!"

"How'd I do?" I asked, not yet showing my anger.

"You were good...much better than most...you know the business; you know your stuff and you were pretty tough in defending yourself." Cheshire cat grin stuck in place.

"Great," I said, now ready to show my emotion. "Is the *fucking* test over? 'Cause I'm tired and we have a lot of work to do, and I don't need this shit!"

"Yeah, the test is over," he said, still enjoying himself. "We're going to get along just fine."

This role was my first in the executive rank, entitling me to perks, most treasured of which was a company car. I selected a Mustang GT, eight cylinder, dual carb, English racing green. My neighbor, a professor at Duke University, called it the Batmobile.

With the trappings, of course, came increased responsibility. There would be little down time in this role, little distinction between personal life and work life. Eric was reputed to be a "frustrated HR person." That is, he took his leadership seriously enough to try to do some of the functions that HR liked to do on its own. I was happy to have a strong partner, rather than a compliant client.

Eric was well aware of the stressful climate and highly opinionated that the environment impacted effectiveness in significant ways. He wanted to take it head on. We did it all: employee opinion surveys, skip level meetings, 360-feedback, team-building sessions, leadership offsites, competency models, even mandated diversity training. Yet, progress was slow. We had to overcome cynicism, and to a certain extent, embedded leadership behaviors. Eric struggled with the dilemma of his own authenticity. Never shy, he would answer truthfully when asked about power and politics, the closed-door struggles that crippled cooperation. Yet, he'd preach teamwork incessantly. He was always an advocate for the customer, and that won the hearts and minds of those who worked for him. I captured Eric's Credo on a PowerPoint chart and carried it around with me:

When you have to make a decision, you should answer these questions, in this order:
1. What is the best thing for the customer?
2. What is the best thing for Northern Telecom as a whole?
3. What is the best thing for Customer Service?
4. And, finally, what is best for me/my department?

It was Eric's belief that too many managers had the order backward, worrying first about themselves and lastly about the customer. He lived by these new rules and expected others to as well.

I learned that it is the leader's *behaviors* that people pay attention to. All of the investments in tools, programs, training, processes, and offsites are sub-optimized if the behaviors are not aligned!

Meanwhile, on an arrogant roll in my parallel universe, I alienated a major segment of the HR population. HR was constantly reorganizing and redefining the functions as we downsized. I seemed to have a permanent role on succeeding transition teams. The only constant we could rely on was change.

I promulgated the Novation's staff support model, delineating two types of staff roles[7]: Business Necessity, or Core Capabilities (Compensation, Benefits, Employee Relations, and Information Services) and Value Added Support (OD), thereby insulting the bulk of the HR population. Trying to defend the position that the world-class way in which we performed the business necessity work laid the foundation for the value added work that might bring competitive advantage was way too little and way too late.

Getting out of the functional OD role and into the generalist roles had been liberating. I was attached to individual businesses, able to form meaningful and strong relationships with business leaders. On more than one occasion, a client introduced me this way, "Tim's my HR guy, but he's not a typical HR guy." Knowing he meant it as a compliment, I finally asked for an explanation. "Well,

---

7 *Real-Time Strategy*, pp. 88–91

you know more about the business than most HR folks, and you're not afraid to challenge us." I was flattered and disappointed at the same time, having become self-important; expecting the rest of the function to become more like me.

I developed a working model for successful HR work: Start out by doing whatever it takes to get invited to the business table. Leverage networks, do favors, use bosses, but get invited to the meetings where business decisions were made. Once at the table, demonstrate understanding of the business issues by mastering the language and the concepts. Add value at the table by asking questions that nobody else asks, but have them be business questions. Affect their thinking. Avoid giving advice. Lead the witnesses, but let them get to the conclusions on their own. In private, win their trust by being a good listener. Never betray their confidence. Never be a spy for senior management or any other boss system. Do not become a therapist. None of this was rocket science, merely an extension of Ulrich's research. But all of it was validated by client feedback.

Above all, I tried to drive out the fear. So many executives and managers were afraid. They were afraid to take risks, talk back to their boss, and have their own opinions. Part of the role of a generalist is to help execs leave the company when their time had come. For many, departure felt like punishment and failure. This eventuality handcuffed so many into caution, and fear. I worked hard to help reposition it as a time that their perceived value-add had come to an end.

There had been no training for this, no corporate programs, but the work was critical. I tried to help those who were encouraged to leave to see that they had choice. They could stay and fight, or they could negotiate terms. But it was important for them to choose how to play it. No one ever got fired outright, and many negotiated new roles with new bosses in new parts of the business. Pass the turkey was practiced at all levels, all the time. For those who couldn't land, it helped that the severance packages were generous.

For many, I had to be direct in my questioning. "Just what are you afraid of?"

"I have a wife and a mortgage, and kids to put through college."

"So? Do you not believe in yourself? Do you not believe that you can get a job elsewhere? The only thing they can do to you, the worst thing they can do to you, is to ask you to leave. Why would you want to stay somewhere that doesn't value you?"

PART 2

ADDING VALUE

CHAPTER 7

TELECOMMUNICATIONS ACT OF 1996

From the time I had joined BNR, in 1984, right through the early '90s, the business language of my clients had been technology- and product-focused. ISDN (Integrated Services Digital Networks) was going to change everything, they said. On our Displayphone terminals, you could get voice and data at the same time, have a conversation with someone while looking at shared material. Watching the data—just words organized into sentences, a memo for example—scroll down the screen at 300 baud was revolutionary, no matter how ancient and slow that looks today. Voice Recognition was being invented in our Montreal lab. DSL (Digital Subscriber Loop) was going to enable data to be transmitted over telephone lines.

For a company that had been a successful manufacturer for its first one hundred years, it became clear that the value add of our products was increasingly delivered by software, rather than the metal frames, wires and circuit boards we routinely shipped all over the world. Even so, for a while, the language had stayed product focused, be it Meridian Information Systems that provid- ed packet transport or the family of DMS telephone switches from Centrex through SupeNode connectors. We had a huge celebra- tion for the release of BCS-17 (Batch Change Supplement—the rather bland generic name for the switch firmware upgrades, that over the years amounted to millions of lines of code, that were released every eighteen months or so).

As the digital age increasingly spread to all aspects of telecommunications, I began to hear more about transmission technology. This industry was going to be led by the companies that could transfer data most efficiently, reliably, and, of course, the fastest. All sorts of possibilities were being developed, many attempting to leverage existing infrastructure: not just the phone lines, but also the cable television networks and even the existing electrical wiring in our houses. A new technology utilizing fiber optics (long strands of glass no thicker than a human hair that served as waveguides, light pipes if you will, to transmit beams of light from end to end) promised to be the most effective as they delivered Synchronous Optical Networks (SONET). Our OC-48 would eventually take 90 percent of the market.

Under the leadership of John Roth, we were one of the first companies to create the wireless[1] market. I was amazed one day to see Rod walking in the parking lot with what looked like an oversized telephone handset up to his ear—he was walking around, talking on the phone. The future was here. Even if I did not understand all the arguments about GSM, CDMA, TDMA, etc., I knew they were about the regulatory standards that were being adopted in different parts of the world, and that these decisions would define the technology paths that we needed to invest in.

A lot of this business language began to change in the mid-90s. More and more the business discussions that drove budget decisions and R+D investments began to be about *customers*, instead of technology or products. If the AT+T divestiture had been the strategic inflection point that enabled Nortel to grow the North American market, the Telecommunications Act of 1996 enabled us to expand exponentially[2]. We were now hitting numbers quarterly

---

1 Larry Macdonald, *Nortel Networks*, pp. 161–174.

2 For an in-depth study of the telecoms industry during this period, see Koss, W.R., *Six Years That Shook The World*.

that we had hit annually just a few years before, with revenues rising to almost $11 billion in 1995.

The Act was intended to bust the telecoms market wide open by allowing free and open competition across all sectors of the industry. Of course, the birth of the Internet also changed paradigms, not the least of which was the potential to bypass embedded traditional networks. The Act even allowed companies to lease part of their networks from other companies, and the concept of a virtual network arose. This was a revolutionary concept in and of itself. Many of these companies needed help understanding their own potential and building business models that would lead to commercial success, and eventually self-sustaining markets. Nortel had the intellectual capital to help them. We certainly had some of the best network engineers in the world. We had to figure out the best way to do so.

My clients' conversations were about both new customers and new kinds of customers. Switching had become quite profitable outfitting the RBOCs (the large Regional Bell Operating Companies that emerged out of divestiture, like Nynex and BellSouth.) But new business models were being developed to compete with them in local markets and to compete with AT+T in the long haul carrier market. (We show our age if we truly remember the time when it was routine to acknowledge, and respect, "I'm on a long-distance call.") How were we going to help new breeds of customers (IOCs— Independent Operating Companies, IXCs—Interexchange Carriers, CLECs—Competitive Local Exchange Carriers; only a few of many examples)? And all these new companies: MCI, WorldCom, Sprint, Quest, UUNET, MFS Communications, and many, many more. Not to mention new end-user business models for Internet access and data applications, led by companies like Netscape, America Online, Excite, and @Home! Finally, we had the opportunity to continue our expansion globally. We now had the technology, the products, the intelligence, the customer satisfaction, and the reach to become a true multinational giant.

Koss[3] argues that John Roth was one of the intellectual operating leaders in a Thought Leadership Model. That is, he was among those who were defining the parameters of how the world of telecommunications was going to be restructured after the revolutions spurred by the Internet and optical technology. John laid out a vision, Webtone[4]. One of the traditional values of POTS (Plain Old Telephone Service) was reliability. When you picked up a handset from a phone, you immediately got dial tone and your calls were always clear and uninterrupted. During the mid-90s, the Internet was still excruciatingly slow and data drops were common. We had lists of Telenet (one of the first commercial packet-switched networks) phone numbers programmed into our personal computers. If one number kept failing, we'd try another. John wanted to make the Internet just as reliable as the phone network, and just as fast.

To accomplish Webtone, and since "the Internet changes everything," he imagined a "culture of speed" with his Right Angle Turn[5]. He described our traditional market as one with long product development and long product life cycles. This was fine for the capital intensive, long-range planning practices of the large infrastructure companies like the RBOCs. But the new customers, the new markets, the data world would demand short product development and short product lifecycles. Indeed, to thrive in the fast-paced environment of the Internet, we would have to develop an "entrepreneurial spirit." Not an easy task for a behemoth.

To succeed in such a world, it might be too slow to *develop* all the capabilities that would be needed. John began to acquire companies to get their capabilities, technologies, and market channels. He also knew that the new world was going to need new business

---

3 Ibid., p.73

4 Macdonald, pp. 175–186.

5 Ibid., p. 178

models, and that we would need a new leadership system and a new company culture.

As John elevated through the ranks from head of North America to president and CEO of the whole company, I had the opportunity to facilitate many change projects that were intended to have Nortel become the unequivocal leader of this new world of telecommunications, to deliver on the Webtone vision. This section is intended to highlight and explain a few of those projects, some successful, some not so much; both to illustrate how directly and intensely we understood the *need* to change, as well as to point out some of those inflection points where we *missed the opportunity* to do so.

CHAPTER 8

NOM IS A DIRTY WORD

At a Marketing Operations staff meeting, while I was the HR director, Sherwood Robbins, the vice-president, introduced a new member of the cabinet. Graham, relocating from Canada, would report directly to Gerry Butters, the president of Northern Telecom, Inc., the US holding company for marketing and sales. But he would be reporting into the region for "care and feeding." It sounded like he was in charge of a project called NAM. All the business leaders around the table seemed to know what "NAM" was, but I was thinking, "This guy's working on Vietnam?" Funny how close some of the parallels would be.

I walked around the cabinet after every business meeting, dropping in on each of the hard-walled offices, to get a real-time fix on the reactions and concerns. After that meeting, the product marketing VP told me about "NAM," or, as he corrected me, NOM, Network Order Management, an attempt to simplify the entire process required to complete a complex network order. "It's a pet project of Gerry's." Gerry Butters was one of the most prominent, legendary execs who had helped build Northern Telecom's stature in North America. He was beloved in the truest sense of the word. "Graham and Gerry go way back. They were in Bellville together, years ago. You better help him," he advised me, "because he doesn't understand that he has problems."

"What kind of problems?" I asked.

"There's no marketing strategy for this thing. Everyone believes Gerry will do the right thing for customers. But there's no marketing strategy." His demeanor was stern, dead serious.

The "problems" were becoming common knowledge around the company. There was no commercial strategy, no understanding of the value proposition to customers. No one was quite *sure* how NOM was going to make money for Nortel, nor how it would satisfy the customers, many of whom had been expressing anxiety every time they heard about it. It was one of those big, hairy, audacious goals[1]. Since everyone respected and believed in Gerry, no one *publicly* questioned the premise. But behind closed doors, I heard nothing but concerns.

At the time, we were still trailing global industry stalwarts like Lucent, Alcatel, and Ericsson. The common belief was that there would have to be significant consolidation in the telecom equipment sector. We needed to slim down our cost structure. Layoffs had already begun. We had even closed a few plants. Manufacturing execs had begun to hope that NOM would be a way to take costs out of the business. The operations leaders had gotten very good at taking cost out of manufacturing processes, but they had begun receiving diminishing returns in their cost reduction efforts. Now they were looking at other functions' processes to see if they could help. The manufacturing execs were, almost to a person, highly critical, judgmental, and distrusting of leaders from other functions, especially marketing. They couldn't imagine that anyone else cared about costs the way that they did.

And, after all, it was Marketing, year over year, who had conditioned the customer to expect price reductions. For example,

---

1 *Built to Last: Successful Habits of Visionary Companies*, Jim Collins and Jerry I. Porras, 1994.

consider line cards, those printed circuit boards that tie your phone to the central office and the rest of the world. When digital switching first came on line in the late '70s, line cards for the DMS-100, the workhorse of the digital multiplexing switching family, were over $100 each. The phone companies ordered millions of these over the years and the company blossomed. But, each year, the price came down. By the mid-90s, line cards were selling for under $10.

The first time I met with Graham, I liked him right away. He's colorful and charismatic, with a big bushy red beard and blond hair, energetic, always wired. I said, "I want to understand NOM better. Who's the client?" A standard OD opening, the "making entry" question. Many projects bog down if the change leader is unclear who the client is, that is, who is going to receive the value as a result of this change. He turned to his computer and pulled up various presentations. Like other execs, he liked to converse through PowerPoint charts. He had very impressive artwork and creative concepts. If nothing else, I could see that he was a chart master. But, he didn't fully answer my question.

After hearing his spiel, I proffered, "By the way, after the staff meeting, I heard some chatter about NOM. I heard resistance, urgency, anxiety; almost fear about how bad it is going to fail." I had to get through the "who said what" stuff by letting him know that I never revealed sources. His attitude was dismissive: "I don't have to give a shit about that. Anyone that has a problem with NOM is resistant to change. They're afraid; they don't understand. I work for Gerry. These guys are just jealous."

NOM attracted high levels of emotion and passion, from both supporters and detractors. I started navigating the learning curve to understand what this project was about, did a lot of listening to a lot of executives, and became an informal coach to Graham, just by virtue of stopping in his office, which happened to be next to mine. We had plenty of off-topic things to talk about to establish a friendly relationship. After a few months, he started to trust me. He began to ask, almost off-handedly, "What are you hearing these days?" The resistance from his peers had grown palpable, and he realized he was dependent on them to actually *implement* NOM. He wanted advice on how to better influence them.

Then, as they say, the world changed. Gerry left the company, soon to join our biggest rival, Lucent. Graham's protector, his mentor, his sponsor, his old friend was gone. A company-wide reorganization followed. Some of the sales functions were split up and folded into separate product groups. There would be no central authority to help implement.

Graham turned pale when he heard the news, saying bluntly, "I'm screwed. What the hell am I gonna do?" His entire implementation strategy had been dependent on Gerry dictating the marching orders through the command-and-control hierarchy.

"Well, you know," I said, "what you're going to do is get back to basics. You're going to figure out what's in it for the customer. You might have to redefine who your clients and stakeholders are." It was in this reorganization that I moved to Customer Service, relocating to another building. It wasn't *convenient* to coach him anymore. I didn't bump into him and he was no longer my client. But relationships transcend organizations. He kept calling me, kept e-mailing me, trying to figure out what was going on. He was anxious about whom he would report to, afraid it might be Manufacturing or, even worse, Finance. I worried that I might be the only safety valve he had.

I made a call to the Switching HR prime, who told me it would be Marketing Operations. Graham called to thank me, believing I had pulled some behind-the-scenes "pass interference," ascribing to me credit I did not deserve. I was growing fond of the perception of having power and did not dissuade him. I liked when executives would come to me and ask for help. That part of the role was flattering—these big, powerful business leaders asking for favors, or delegating organizational tasks. They trusted HR to do the right thing for the right reasons. Or, of course, they were often just playing me, as Neal had predicted.

As his first order of business after the announcement, Sherwood held a project review and discovered that all the milestones were being missed. He held a budget review and discovered just how far the project was overextended. He updated Gedas Sakus, the president of Switching, and they decided to insert one of the regional sales VPs over Graham. Sales had their own vision of what NOM could be. In fact, the definition of NOM was always fluid, always changing. There was no historical record, no archive, and most of us were too busy to remember all of the detail, so trust was implied and could easily be abused. When challenged, Graham used to say, "Don't worry about it. Me and Gerry know what we're doing."

Meanwhile, Eric started pushing me to get more involved in NOM. He was aware of prior relationships. He heard from customers about issues, and he was pushing me to help fix them. I attended NOM reviews. Eric wanted NOM to simplify things for the customer. His metaphor lampooned the process that the customer used to order switching products, centered on the CI (customer information) form:

"Picture yourself getting a catalog in the mail the size of the New York City White Pages, with ten thousand piece parts. You have to order a car by picking out all the parts you need for the car, down to the switches and wires. And you have to make sure that the pieces you choose can be engineered together. That's the burden on you. That's all your problem as you fill out this CI form."

Some people wanted to call the project SOM, for Simplified Order Management. Throw most of the catalog out, reduce the number of parts customers can order and offer them models instead. "We should stop selling parts and sell models." Unfortunately, it belied the complexity of the established base of installed networks and raised serious commercial issues. You cannot rip out networks and replace them with models. Over time, networks become organic as they change and grow. New products were "added on." After several months in this structure, Gedas came to Raleigh for an all-day project review. As the VP was presenting Gedas said, "I don't like these numbers." It was still costing way too much.

"Well Gedas, this is what the numbers are!"

Gedas put down his pen and lowered his glasses to the end of his nose. He looked at the nervous exec and said, "You're not listening to me. I don't like these numbers, and if you don't bring me numbers that I like, I will find somebody else who will."

For the next couple of project reviews, the numbers looked better. But the annual budget was due and the numbers were way off again. It appeared that the Sales VP had been misrepresenting reality. He was quietly encouraged to leave, and he talked to me on his way out. "What else was I supposed to do?" he asked sincerely.

"Tell the truth."

Sherwood called to ask me to put together a key resource list, or "slate," to find a new leader for the project.

"I'm not your HR guy."

"Yeah, but you know the players, the process; you know what I need." I called his HR person for permission, who said, "Be my guest." I interviewed for about two months, talking to five key resources. To a person, each one said something like, "You're crazy! Nobody would take this job. This job is a no-win situation. The last guy got fired and Graham is not getting it done. You'd have to be nuts. This is a career-derailing job."

When I reported back to Sherwood, he smiled a little. "You could do this job."

I laughed out loud. "The previous guy got fired, the expert is floundering, and five KRs from the line have told me no. I love a challenge. Let me think about it."

My title would be AVP, North American NOM Implementation. Out of staff and into the line. A chance to interact directly with customers. Originally, NOM was supposed to be a twelve-month project, but it was now going into its third year. My charge was to *implement*. I wanted to talk to a lot of stakeholders to see whether or not the project was still feasible. Was there any coherent vision at all? Was there enough common ground among my sponsors that I could succeed? Was there any belief that there really was something to implement?

I also knew I would need support from all these other functions, so I wanted to demonstrate trust and respect in advance. If they were advisors on my decision to take the job, then they would already be enrolled in helping me with the solution.

First, I called my straight-line HR boss, Don, who said, "Hey, jobs in the line are great. Great career development. Don't worry about it. Can't hurt your career. Whatever happens you'll learn a lot, probably do a lot, and you're welcome back in HR. So it's not career limiting for you; go do it. Make us proud." I trusted Don, so I felt like I had a safety valve.

Next, I called my client, Eric, and he said, "It's about time they came to their senses. You gotta do this. Go."

Then I went to see the heads of Manufacturing, Finance, and Technology, most of the people who had been complaining about NOM. They expressed some doubts in the project, but helped me build my confidence. "Why do you think I can do this?" I asked each one.

"Because people on both sides of the issue trust you. You'll get to the truth and you'll do what's right." That was it? That was my capability? The ability to not play a political power game with the project?

The common ground that emerged from all the conversations was that NOM was a good idea. It *should* be good for the customer. It *would* be good for the manufacturing process. It would be smart to implement it. There was also some sympathy and awareness about the political dynamics: that this had been a pet project, and that it was victimized when Gerry left.

While I was busy considering this opportunity, several HR executives were documenting what we had learned in transforming the HR function[2]. I had come to believe our own press. Our implementation of HR as a business partner, helping to formulate and implement business strategy, helping to govern the company, was a pioneering effort.

I accepted the offer and took my first line job telling myself, "I'm going to apply all this OD stuff I'm promulgating. Stop coaching and learning and start doing. I'm going to have councils and shared leadership. I'll be a good communicator, listen to the people, and have skip-level meetings. I'm going to be an exemplary leader." I established a multi-tiered governance structure. I created a board of directors that was a cross-functional council, and I had a separate implementation council. Subgroups in my team had process councils at the working levels.

I was operating under two beliefs. One was that it would be important to drive decisions down to the people who had the best knowledge to make them. My second core belief was that if I led by rallying around the customers, then I could trust employees to make the best decisions, because they would have the knowledge and a supportive environment. The governance was my way of creating such an environment for the project.

My new bosses and clients loved this theorist view of governance, but I started drowning in a deluge of meetings. My direct staff met every Tuesday from seven in the morning until seven at night. That was the schedule. If we ran over, we stayed until nine, ten, even eleven o'clock at night. Whatever it took. We all just went at it, solving issues making decisions, and working on tasks as if we all had a clear, agreed-to picture of the goal we were working

---

2   "Rearchitecting the Human Resources Function at Northern Telecom," Jim Kochanski and Phil Randall, *Human Resources Management Journal*, Summer, 1994, pp. 299–315.

toward. I had articulated objectives for myself and shared them with the teams:

Objective 1: Learn the process

My early objective was to learn how network order management operated. I went around asking people for definitions of NOM, to find the common ground among the implementers and clients. I discovered pretty quickly that I wasn't clever enough to learn all the details of the end-to-end process. It was too complex and there were too many facets.

When I had this conversation with Graham, he said, "It's not that you're not smart enough or clever enough. You just realize how big it is. My downfall is that I'm trying to do everything. I'm trying to be *the* decision-maker. I try to keep the whole thing, end to end, in my head, and I think I get it. But then I turn my back for a moment, do some work over here, and it all flows away down there."

The Center for Creative Leadership was developing a model (DIM) in which leadership can be thought of as evolving from Dominance (where the leader *instructs* people what to do) to Influence (where the leader *influences* the team about the direction to take) to Meaning-Making (where the leader *participates with* the team in figuring out what to do). In the dominance style of leadership that pervaded Nortel, you had to be able to answer any question that came up. I'd watched it so many times. If you can't answer a question when you're up with your chart deck, and you have to ask one of your staff, you're considered weak. You don't know your process; you don't know your project: *you* should know the detail. How else can you make decisions? I was going to take the risk of being overly dependent on my staff. I was going to become a great leader, not a great process person, or even a great project manager. I stuffed my head with this fluff.

I collected issues, prioritizing them in terms of implementation impact and effect on the budget. I asked my staff to detail an end-to-end process flow. "From the trigger to the deliverable; take me through it." I knew we were spending the bulk of the money on information technology, new tools, new databases, and new processes. I wanted to see how it all added up. There was a team in a room for a week. They papered the walls with a blank roll of newsprint and started flow-charting. The diagram went around three walls. You had to walk it to experience it. You had to experience it to understand it.

I was working six or seven days each week, from twelve to fourteen hours a day. Each day was an endless series of meetings with staff, clients, stakeholders, and customers. Many were coming to me to complain about the project, to complain about people on the project. There was always a lot of blaming going on, a lot of fear bubbling below the surface.

Graham had been directing a cross-functional implementation team. Originally, he didn't try to lead; he tried to dominate. He naively assumed that when he produced "the solution," all of the upstream and downstream organizations would adapt to it. He had thought the backing of the sales president would be all the convincing he would need. As it turned out, the resistance was genetically encoded by the potential impact on the people. If NOM were successful, some of the groups would no longer be needed. There was no incentive for folks to work themselves out of their jobs, no safety nets for those who did.

My theory was to shift leadership from a dominance principle to a "making meaning" leadership style. I wanted to include, somehow, representatives from every group that touched this process. I thought if they worked on the decisions together, they would more naturally help implement it.

I spent a couple of weeks living on planes, going to talk to each sales region. It was on one of these trips that I first met Clarence, who was running CALA (Caribbean and Latin America). He and I hit it off and he seemed genuinely grateful that I had made the trip. None of my predecessors had been to ask him about NOM.

I even got to meet directly with customers in a few of the regions, one of whom wanted to meet with me without the sales reps in the room. She was a fan of NOM, but anxious to invest in it, afraid we might pull the plug on it prematurely. One of the major accounts vice-president said, over a drink, "I'm all for this model idea. In fact we will define the models for you." But then we discovered that their models wouldn't work for other customers.

The scariest thing I had to learn about was the budget. I had a terrific finance person assigned to me, and I asked her to run some numbers. As near as we could document, we had already spent at least $68 million[3]. We had some new tools, but no real output, no measurable value. I still could not get end-to-end data flow.

Objective 2: Enroll the staff

My parallel objective at the beginning was to get the employees to trust me. I had about four hundred people in my organization. Early in the project, I had negotiated a couple of severance packages and asked a couple of people to look for jobs elsewhere. These were good people who had been victimized by the situation. Naturally, there was a lot of fear and a lot of distrust of management. The prevailing attitude was that executives were idiots. "If they would stop changing the leaders around, we could finish this project and deliver to the customer. And now we've got an HR guy running the project! How do I get out?"

So I started running lots of "skip-level" meetings. The theory was that part of leadership is determining how leaders/managers in your organization are motivating and developing employees. Employees are afraid, often, to tell the truth when their boss is in the room. Bosses fear they will be exposed as inadequate. It's hard to get at the "truth" with so many walls. So my NOM skip-levels were

---

3 Several staff members believed that number was way too conservative, knowing that a lot of bodies had been assigned "on loan," while their time was charged to other projects. These people believed that the true cost to date was closer to one hundred million US dollars.

small meetings of ten or so people, held over breakfast or lunch. The group's manager reported to me but wasn't in the room. It was the employees' chance to tell me how things were going and what they needed from me.

I held a monthly GIS (General Information Session) to which I invited all the project staff in a particular geography. In Raleigh, there were two hundred and fifty people, of which about two hundred would come out to the meetings. I pledged to tell them the truth. There had been some sense that leaders had been stonewalling, not telling what they knew. We had some rather lengthy GISs, as I patiently hung in there, doing my best to answer each and every question, even the disrespectful, angry ones.

I also leveraged any and all prior relationships that I could count on—ex-clients, former subordinates and ex-bosses—to help me spread the word that I would listen and could be trusted. I knew I was only as good, or as strong, as the sum total of the relationships I had cultivated over time.

Objective 3: Project Planning

After meeting with corporate auditors from Toronto, I agreed to install the Information Systems (IS) Gate Process, which was supposed to be all about discipline, hitting dates, meeting milestones, delivering customer requirements. It was a hybrid of the BNR development process that, unfortunately, also attracted some of the permissive culture. There was usually no penalty for being late. We started over, cobbled together a Gate 0A, a definition of the project, describing it in a language that product sponsors and others would understand.

We did a test case, putting a mock order through the process. It's the idea of stapling yourself to an order to test the process, but do it in virtual time to find out where the glitches and stops are. We still couldn't get end-to-end data flow.

Yet, there were people managing the pieces who were declaring their tool and their module done. When I asked, "Why can't I get data flow through your module?" they would blame the guy upstream. Paradoxically, they worried not one iota about the impact of their module downstream. That's when I engaged some consultants. Both were external contractors who had been doing process and tools work. I broke the prevailing practice and just added them to my leadership team, welcoming them to participate in decision-making discussions. They had been doing grunt work, but each had much higher levels of capability. They provided me with fresh, above board intelligence from an outside perspective. They had no axes to grind and never talked about individuals, only processes.

With their guidance, I started holding IS ops reviews and discovered that there was no consistency, no agreement on tools, and approaches across multitudes of IS sub-functions. For example, there was a high level agreement in NOM to use object-oriented programming so we could reuse modules. But I learned that we needed to be more specific than, "Use object-oriented programming." There are many different languages and flavors of object-oriented programming. One reason we couldn't get end-to-end data flow was because some components were developed in different languages. The boss over one tool might have decided that C+ was the language to use. Yet he has to get inputs from another group that might have decided to use vanilla UNIX. And he has to give outputs to another group that might have decided to use C++. I was absolutely flummoxed. I regressed, reverted to the prevailing blame culture. I talked about other people. In my staff meetings, I blamed IS. My behavior spread a great deal of fear. So much for my leadership theory.

I was summoned to Toronto to update Gedas. When he had agreed to my appointment, he had said, "In three months I want you to come tell me what's wrong with NOM, what caused it, who do I blame, and what do I have to do to fix it." It was time to deliver on my commitment. I wore my best suit. He was cordial and polite, always the ultimate gentleman. "Come on in, let's have a cuppa coffee. Let's sit over here on the sofa and you tell me what you found."

"Well, Gedas, I promised I'd tell you where the problem started."

"Oh yes, do you have that?" and he sat back.

"Yeah, and it starts at the top. Even you're a part of the problem."

I didn't soften the blow because I really felt that what I had discovered was such an indictment of leadership that I was going to let him have it. I needed him to take some accountability because I would need strong demonstration of new leadership if I were going to turn this thing around, to get the employees trusting management again.

"You have to understand that if you go to a meeting and you say, 'Bring me numbers I like or I'll get someone who will,' you're threatening someone's career and people start to make bad decisions. They act out of fear."

Then I said, "It's not just leadership, of course. I have a serious IS problem. I have a customer expectations problem. Remember that Gerry started this as a customer value exercise and now you have turned it into a cost reduction exercise. As a cost reduction exercise it's going to get too far away from the customer."

"I think it can be both," he countered. "I think you're wrong, Tim. *Of course* it's a cost reduction. Have you not seen our manufacturing numbers and our margins? Everything is a cost reduction exercise."

"Well, but the people who do grunt level work, this is what they mean when they say they need vision. They have a whole mental model, Gedas, when something is a cost-reduction exercise versus a customer value exercise. I think there are different capabilities, different people, different motivations…"

By the end of the meeting he said, "I'll choose to disagree with you that it can't be both; but if you want to know what's primary, it's primarily a cost reduction exercise. But do it in such a way that it satisfies the customers."

I ran out of counter-arguments, capitulated, respecting both him and his position. "Thanks for your time."

I hadn't used a single PowerPoint chart. It was an engaging conversation. I was feeling good at the end of it; that I could work for him; that he met the leadership style I had hoped for, by not throwing me out of his office or threatening to get someone else.

Suspiciously soon after my meeting with Gedas, John Roth called me and asked, "What do you think of Sherwood?" When I had been considering whether to take this role, John, at the time president of North America, was one of the people I had asked for advice. He had been president of BNR when I joined the company, and I had followed his career, impressed at his ability to get results. I knew him a little bit, as he occasionally met with the senior HR team. He had encouraged me to take the role.

"Excuse me, John? You know, he's my boss. He's good at marketing. He's good at marketing operations. He respects the customer. I've sat in his staff meetings; I've sat in his regional calls. When you need them, he produces numbers for you out of a hat. He single-handedly creates software buyouts. He's a good leader." Not even a hint of a negative thought crossed my mind. "What is this about, John?"

"I don't think he's the right guy for this NOM thing. It's a mess. I'm gonna move it. How do you feel about that?"

"Um, are you taking it away from me?"

"Moving you with it."

"Well," I said, "I've got a rapport going with Sherwood and I think he's got the customer in mind. What's your motivation to move me? It's probably going to slow me down to get a new boss." I was borderline babbling; both flattered to have my opinion asked for and nervous about whom I would be reporting to.

"Are you afraid to have a new boss?"

"No, I'm not afraid to have a new boss." Should I be? "I'm trying to understand. Are you going to move me to Gedas, because I think that'll be fine?"

"No, Gedas is too busy; that's too high up. I'm going to move you to Peter." Peter Worsley was the head of Manufacturing. The most senior person in Raleigh, he and I had worked together on the Raleigh Leadership Council. I had absolute respect for him and trusted him implicitly. But I also knew how he felt about NOM. He had not been sure that I should take the role.

"John, Peter's been mostly negative about this. He thinks that Marketing has screwed it up."

He laughed, "At least you're well connected."

Sherwood was angry. "This is bull, Tim. This is John punishing me for others' screw ups." But, ever the consummate professional, he recovered quickly. "Just go tell Peter the truth and I'll try to help you out."

Peter and I had known each other for a lot of years. Even so, we clashed immediately. In our first one-on-one meeting, he asked questions about the specs. The answers were six layers below me and I couldn't answer them. He accused me of being a weak leader, saying, "You're out of your element. It was a gutsy move for an HR guy to take something like this on, but you don't know what's going on. Why don't you admit you can't do this?"

"Peter, I'm practicing a different leadership style, that's all. It's this new thing…*I trust my staff*. I don't second-guess them constantly. I think my value add is making sure we're working on the right project, make sure there's customer value, make sure I have a budget, make sure I have the right resources and create meaning for the people so they know what they're working on. I think I *am* a good leader. I don't think I need to know every piece of detail that you ever want to hear."

He didn't blow me off. We scheduled an ops review, and he got at the detail he wanted. Afterward, in his office, he asked me, "What do you think we should do?"

"I think we should finish the project. But I think we need to get clear about the fact that it's not ready to *implement*."

I went back to my team and I said, "Overturn every rock. I want every spider exposed, every snake uncovered, every ghost released. I want to know everything we have to overcome. Tell me *exactly* what it will take to finish this project."

I had heard about an underground newsletter called *Brave New World*, buried on a NOM server. I was able to print the complete set of back issues, about a year's worth, just a couple of typed pages each. It was insightful, funny, biting satire, yet hopeful. It was a little disrespectful of management and leadership, but it was telling the truth about what was going on.

The name of the editor was kept secret. The running spoof in it was, "I wrote this article last month about our leaders and I didn't get fired again." I leaked to my management team, and anyone else who would listen, that I would like to meet the editor.

She self-identified, just showed up in my office one day, and said, "I hear you're looking for me?"

"I like your chutzpah. I admire your commitment to the project. I'd like to use the channel." I started feeding her intelligence.

At the end of the next GIS meeting, she surprised me by coming on stage and presenting me with an engineer's hat, saying, "The people from the organization would like to award you with this hat because we trust you to drive the train."

I had a surprise in return. "I've been reading *Brave New World*. It's a pretty neat publication. I desperately wanted to know who the editor was. I discovered that all the employees knew but no one would tell me. But I found out." And there was this big hush that came over the room. "I found out and I have a thousand-dollar Award of Excellence reward here. So, Michelle, come back up." There was a standing ovation as we hugged on stage.

As I approached the end of six months as a line manager, John called again. Not to wish me a happy anniversary. "I want a few folks to review your implementation plan. Set up a meeting in RTP, within two weeks, and show it to Peter, Eric, and Alan[4]. Make a go/ no-go recommendation, and *they'll decide.*"

I had hired an engineer from Bell Atlantic's Purchasing division to help bring the customer view to the project team. He opened the review with a demonstration that capital expenditure planning processes at the large Telco's were changing. They could no longer operate in a world where time was a luxury, where they could plan their purchases three years out. The exponential growth of data communications was changing everything. Soon, cable television providers would become competitors, offering broadband service to businesses. He argued that the customer *needed* the network ordering processes to be simplified. We then shifted to the project, giving true pictures of the process problems, the tools problems, and the commercial issues. I presented a detailed action plan and a suggested budget, making the case to implement: it would take another year and another $20 million.

We had started at 8:00 a.m., and it was now about 6:00 p.m. Although exhausted, I was convinced we had sold the plan. Eric spoke first, "Do you want to thank your staff and meet with us in private?"

---

4 Alan Fraser was the corporate vice-president for Strategic Planning. I had never met him, had seen him only on videoconferences. I had heard that he thought we were throwing good money after bad.

"No," I said without hesitation. "This is my leadership team. Let's have the conversation with them in the room." We had another hours' discussion until every question they had was answered in the appropriate detail.

Peter said, "Thanks, Tim, and thanks to your team. Give the three of us about fifteen minutes and then come to my office. When I got there, he did not hesitate, "You've been very thorough. And very realistic. But the answer is no. You can't have a year to implement." Clearly, I guessed, they had their marching orders from John. "Come back in a week with a plan to implement within six months. And bring it in at five million."

For the next week, we worked around the clock. My staff's advice was consistent, if flawed. They said, "We can't implement in six months for five million dollars. But we can put a plan together that makes it look like we can. Then we can slip it."

Enough was enough. In the follow-up meeting, I surprised the execs, disappointing my team, and recommended shutting the project down. They all thought I was making a very brave, gutsy decision, but it was the right decision. One of them said, "Nobody *ever* recommends shutting a project down. Ever. It's not done."

But the decision was easy. I refused to play the game. It wouldn't be right for the customer. It was against my gut. My integrity was on the line. I had been appointed to this role because the executives trusted me. I could not betray that trust.

I understood the fear on the part of my staff. Their jobs were at stake. I was in the boat with them though, going down with the ship, having no idea what I was going to do next. The immediate work was to draft a shut-down plan. "There's still a customer need out there for some of this stuff. Inventory everything and mothball the best pieces. I want a learning history. I want to protect the people from layoffs. There'll be no more NOM as a stand-alone project." The name NOM had become toxic.

As part of the exit plan, I held a funeral. I knew from William Bridges' change book (*Managing Transitions*) that we needed an ending. People would need closure or they would not believe that the project was really over. They would need to get on with their lives and look for the next project. Perhaps, most importantly, they would need to avoid the feeling of failure. It was not their fault. They did not have to be afraid that they would be punished for being on a cancelled project.

There were so many people who had so much *self* invested in NOM, people who had been on it for three years. Together with my HR partner, we knew that we had to do something relevant, yet dramatic. I rented some space at a hotel and draped the room in black. We crafted a mock coffin and invited all the employees who had worked on NOM. We designed it as an open-mike Irish wake, where people could come up and talk about the deceased.

People brought stuff that they needed to let go of. The document for Gate 0A went into the casket first. One woman brought about twelve binders of information. She cried as she threw them all in. People came up and gave testimony, laughed, and wept. Told stories about the deceased. In my eulogy, I encouraged them to remember the metaphor of the *Brave New World*; that it's hard building new worlds. I told them how proud I was to be associated with them, sharing how hard it was for me. I thanked them for the learning, the honesty, and the trust. I had expended a lot of energy, and a bit of my soul, trying to make a difference. Yet, the results weren't apparent at all. The business outcomes were not being achieved.

"Learning is really important to me. I'll never let the company stop learning from NOM." I held that as a guidepost, probably to the point of being obnoxious about it for the next few years. My mantra became, "Let's make sure we get the learning from NOM." I gave away *Brave New World* T-shirts and opened up the bar.

I had people come back to me a number of times over the next five years or so. Every now and then, I would get a phone call from someone who used to be on my staff. Just wanted you to know, we implemented (one of the tools). "We didn't associate it with NOM, and we only implemented about 80 percent of it. But the customer loved it. The issue came up again, the time was right and we got it out of mothballs and implemented it. We're not supposed to let anyone know that it was part of NOM, but we wanted you to know."

Some years later, a woman asked me to be her mentor as part of a formal leadership development program we were offering from HR. When I asked her why, she said, "You were the best leader I've ever seen. Don't you remember that I worked for you in NOM?"

I had met a lot of new people, and some of those people are still good friends. Of course, there were others that I hurt, who have probably never forgiven me. That's all part of the legacy. Change agents don't always get to the destination they set out for, but if we are true to ourselves and stick to our principles, we just might learn something from the journey. Out of it all, I came away with a personal relationship with John Roth, future CEO and master change agent.

CHAPTER 9

90-DAY WONDER

During the process of shutting down NOM, I got to know Alan. In his corporate strategy role, some of the funding for NOM had been billed to his budget. He was glad the bleeding was over, but he wanted to make sure we tied down all the loose ends. At the end of one of our briefing sessions, he completely surprised me when he offered me a job. He wanted me to be his "EA," executive assistant, for a new role he was getting. I refused him, at first, without really thinking about it. My mental model of an EA was a high-level admin, someone who would run his calendar, run his e-mail, run interference. I did not see how it would be fun or how it would advance my career. He kept at me, reformulating the mental model. "You will be my surrogate. You will go to meetings that I can't make, make phone calls that I don't have time for, and you will speak for me. I will not undermine you. You will gain respect, grow some new networks, and learn a ton about the business. Do it for ninety days. Get me started. Then we'll see. Please."

How could I resist? It was not like I had another job lined up. He was announced as the chief marketing officer for Public Switching, reporting to Gedas. But he told me that he had an understanding with John that this was a short term development move, a holding position, that he was being groomed for something bigger, maybe even the next president of Switching. Good to his word, at his first staff meeting, he launched me: "When Tim calls, it's me calling; when Tim makes a decision, it's me making a decision."

The two of us embarked on a whirlwind tour of North America, visiting each major sales region, meeting with each major account vice-president, many over late night dinners. He wore me out. He had an amazing reserve of energy. He thought nothing of a schedule that allowed us only a few hours of sleep each night. We'd go from fancy meals and too much wine with a sales VP one night, to airport hot dogs the next. We arrived at our San Francisco hotel after midnight and were out of it by 4:00 a.m.

We flew into Calgary, rented a car, and he started the drive out to a luxurious ski resort in Banff National Park, deep in the spectacular Canadian Rockies, where the Canadian sales team was having an executive offsite. Bitter cold, snow drifts everywhere, patchy ice on the road, and he asked me to dial in to a conference call. I passed the phone to him so he could lead the call while driving. He was actually presenting from a chart deck while I turned the pages. Speeding down the highway. He veered over to the shoulder while making a point. Frightened, I reached over and pressed his mute button. "Alan, what the fuck are you doing? You're going to get us killed. Pull over and let me drive!"

He calmly released the mute button and said to the call, "Excuse me for just a minute, guys; I have to take care of something." This was the only time I ever saw his temper flare, and it only lasted a moment. He waved the phone at me, raised his voice slightly, saying, "Don't you get it? I have to be in control! I have to control *everything.* Now flip the charts and stop worrying. I know what I'm doing; I've done this a thousand times." He took a breath, now as calm as could be, and went back to the call.

We arrived safely at dusk and parked the car. While walking to the lodge, we saw numerous elk roaming the grounds as the sun set and the moon rose over the mountains. A few seconds of pure beauty and tranquility. Majestic. Of course, five minutes later he was presenting his chart deck and an hour after that we were back in the car. When we got back to Calgary, just before midnight, while the crew up at Banff was finishing the five-course dinner we had been invited to, we drove around for an hour looking for a Swiss Chalet. He wanted some rotisserie chicken. We lived like this for the better part of the first month.

He was sounding out potential models of change, testing ideas on the sales teams. For the previous decade, we had been hearing the same warnings: the cash cow is going to dry up soon. Any day now. For the most part, digital networks were built out and we were living on software enhancements, features, and line cards. Customers waited for good deals, good pricing. It was a buyer's market. Yet, year after year, this business produced the earnings for the company. How long could it last?

Alan believed that we would have to tier our customers, invest significantly in the ones who provided us with profitability, but deemphasize our relationships with those that didn't. Maybe even drop one or two. He believed that he had data that could prove that with certain customers, we continued to lose money. He was influenced by Michael Treacy and Fred Wiersema's new book, *The Discipline of Market Leaders: Choose Your Customers, Narrow Your Focus, Dominate Your Market*. I, too, was stimulated when I read it. It was a profound theory, well-articulated and cogently argued. To the sales team, it was pure heresy: *choose* our customers? *They* choose us.

No matter how logical the argument, I doubted that we would we able to execute. We had no plan to protect the executives and sales teams who sold to the potential second tier. No one worth their salt would want to stay on those accounts if we alienated the customer. The sales teams worked their networks behind the scenes. I could tell by the cautious way they were challenging him in the meetings that they were afraid of him. Afraid to tell him the whole truth, that his approach was a mistake, that they would not support him. I could see the fear in their eyes, in the way they questioned him and the way he brushed aside their concerns. Several trusted me enough to tell me the truth about what they were thinking. Behind closed doors, behind his back, they second-guessed and undermined him.

I tried to tell him what I was observing. "Screw 'em," he said, "they don't have a choice."

That was his ruthless side. The other side of him was soft, caring, and sentimental. He set up a Friday afternoon tea, as he had learned when in London, for the cabinet staff, complete with scones and cucumber sandwiches. His charm was authentic. The admins loved him, even as the sales VPs conspired against him.

The warning shots kept coming. In confidence, execs I trusted told me he was in trouble. He was sure I was worried for nothing. "Bullshit, screw 'em. I have John's backing; that's all I need." But the chatter was so high, so constant, that I sensed he *was* in trouble. The next time I was in Toronto, I carefully broached the subject with John, only to discover that John seemed to be testing him, not yet fully sponsoring him.

That night, over dinner, I asked Alan, "What kind of a contract do you have with John?"

"Back of a napkin. Right here in Toronto, in the company cafeteria. I sketched out my ideas and John told me to go for it."

Whew. Oh, shit. I went over my self-imposed boundary, giving advice when it clearly wasn't asked for. "Alan, you don't have a good contract. It's too weak for what you hope to accomplish. What if John was just being polite, just listening?"

He didn't buy it, kept on task, ignored the chatter. My dilemma was that I absolutely thought that he was right. But his strategy was so brilliant it may have blinded us. The resistance against him mounted. He was not leveraging established executive relationships, not listening to even his friends' concerns. Instead of carefully building alignment, instead of taking another trip out to the regions, instead of listening to his own product owners, he stayed on message, firmly and steadfastly believing in the cause, expecting that John would throw him a rope if he needed one.

And then suddenly he was leaving. He accepted a job as a CEO of a startup, an offer he said he couldn't refuse. He made a big deal of showing me his generous offer letter, almost as if he felt he had to justify himself to me. There was a lot of upside potential for him and it was clearly a great opportunity. I went way over the boundary when I asked him, "Are you fleeing because you are failing?"

"I'm not failing. You don't know what you're talking about."

And then he was gone. But he had met his promise to me. I had learned a ton about the business, strengthened my relationships with the major account vice-presidents and even with the sales executive vice-president, grew some new networks deep in the sales teams and even won some new respect. For ninety days I had been immersed in the front end, with a clear line of sight to customers. Alan taught me so much about the value add of our intellectual capital, our knowledge of networks, and all of our history that was embedded in our customer relationships. He thought it was critical that our development teams understand how to leverage all of that value. He believed that we should not just be selling products, sometimes to customers who could no longer afford them, who may not even be around after the next wave of consolidation. He thought our new practice of financing deals for some of these customers was a big mistake. "We're not a bank," he told me in the middle of the night over a Tim Hortons donut. "If we don't understand our value proposition, we are not going to lead the industry."

Even though there were times when I thought I could read John, there were many others when he was inscrutable. For what it's worth, I did not think he was heartbroken about Alan's departure. I was certainly much more upset, maybe just because I had invested so much of my time and energy into this guy. I argued that it was concerning to me, that it was not the first example of a key talent, a passionate leader, just walking out the front door.

But, I had more important things to worry about, starting with the fact that, once again, I needed a job.

CHAPTER 10

ACCOUNTABILITY

I had been working with senior execs for a number of years and, for the most part, I was disappointed with the leadership theories in use. A number of times we had defined leadership characteristics, but we had never been able to put a program in place that would systematically develop these characteristics or, more importantly, reward for them. The politics of the company were shaped by a palpable lack of trust. Decisions were routinely relegated to potential effects on established power bases. Insecurity was pandemic. A common characteristic I had found among many leaders was self-doubt. The company had grown so fast; there had been so many field promotions. We continuously diluted our talent. Fast growth triggered promotions whether individuals were ready for management or not. Often, the result was that we lost the skills of a great engineer from the field while we gained a weak manager. Too many of them lived in fear that someone would find out about them, find out that they are not really as good as their network purported them to be. The Peter Principle[1] was being lived out on a daily basis.

---

1 Formulated by Dr. Laurence J. Peter: In a Hierarchy Every Employee Tends to Rise to His Level of Incompetence, *The Peter Principle*.

With Alan's departure, I gave serious consideration to leaving. I was astounded at the per diem rate that we regularly paid to numerous external consultants, many who came across as mediocre, at best, in their ability to drive any real change. I imagined that I could make more money, and be less stressed, if I hung out a shingle.

Jenny had become John's HR prime, the senior HR person for North America. She had stayed in touch with me throughout my immersion with Alan. Toward the end of my ninety days, she let me know that she wanted me to come back to HR. My immediate response was an attempt to close that door. "No, I don't think I want to go back to HR. I think I've learned what I'm going to learn from HR."

She urged me to think about it from a different perspective, "I want you to work with me and John." I called her straight line boss, Don, the senior vice-president of HR, for his opinion.

"Tell me why you want to leave."

"I don't like the power politics here."

"Then stay outside them."

"As an external, I could say 'no' to work I didn't think was viable."

"You can say no to work here."

"I think that my personal values are in conflict with the values of HR." Whew. I'd said it.

"Tim, your values are totally aligned with the business and you have absolute integrity. I want you to provide some leadership so that those values permeate throughout all of HR. Tim, let's go through all of what you think the advantages are of being an external, and I'll see what I can do to provide them here." I was flattered at the attention. I guess I was hooked after Don's terrific sell, but I was still being passive-aggressive. Jenny set up a meeting to let John do the last recruiting piece. John was in the space of, "Well, Jenny thinks it will be good. I like what you did with NOM; you have a lot of guts. I need someone who will tell the truth. I need someone who can feel the pulse of the company."

"I won't be your spy."

"That's good; I have enough of them," chuckling a little too easily.

They made me an offer I couldn't refuse: Organization Effectiveness for North America, an individual contributor role, no managing of people, sort of an internal consultant. It would turn out to be my best three years with the company. At the outset, details were scarce. Jenny suggested I take a "gestalt psychology[2]" approach to helping the organization improve. Look at the whole system, the processes, and tease out the patterns. I wanted to find the tipping point[3] in the leadership model that would break the back of the distrust barrier.

"A good place to start," she said, "is this general manager model. It's a large-scale change initiative, and it's stuck."

John had announced a shift to a general manager model about a year earlier, and he wanted to train his GMs. He wanted to help them understand what a GM was, because he didn't think they all knew what he wanted out of them. I had known that the corporate OD group, under Kerry's leadership, had been working to characterize a competency model for a GM. Based on behavioral event interviews, the approach captures the characteristics of those thought to be experts. Practical, rather than theoretical, the technique extracts the success criteria evidenced when the best general managers describe their own success stories. The project team was on track to launch the model at a "General Manager Forum." The team was developing assessment tools to accompany the introduction, assuming that John would want to impose rigor to close the delta between what we had and what he wanted. But there had been a disconnect. John harbored a visceral opposition to many assessment tools. He was not interested in HR's strategy of driving a mandated assessment model into the population.

---

2   Gestalt psychology is a theory of mind and brain that proposes that the operational principle of the brain is holistic, parallel, and analog, with self-organizing tendencies; or, that the whole is different from the sum of its parts.

3   We were inspired by Malcolm Gladwell's original *New Yorker* article, June 3, 1996.

HR had been reluctant to let go of the approach, which they had viewed as a lead application of a best practice. As my entry point, Jenny encouraged me to sit down with John and have a conversation. There was a whole brouhaha around the very *definition* of a GM. Who should even have the title? John wanted job titles changed. "Only *real* GMs can be called GMs." Peeling the onion, layering my questions, I revealed his solution: You're only a GM if you have a true P & L, if you have authoritative marketing responsibility, and you have specific and measurable revenue and earnings goals. The Profit and Loss statement was a symbol of a distinct business, and therefore, whoever owned one was a general manager. A few of the presidents had been using "General Manager" for some leaders of individual product lines, small business segments that did not have separate P&Ls. It was easy to clean up the list by retitling them "Business Managers."

Feeling we were only masking a symptom, I asked him, "John, what is the *intent* of this model? What *business issue* are you trying to fix?" In effect, who's the client?

One hundred percent of his answer was internally focused. "It's about accountability, about responsibility; it's about control." That was what he said, but it was not what I heard. My filter, my mental translator, was interpreting this as, "Who do I blame when things go wrong?"

I was enthralled, having all this time with him, dutifully taking notes, challenging him a little, and having a good conversation. When I got into what the barriers to the model were, he answered, "We're growing so fast, we've named people general managers and they aren't even good business managers. They don't even understand the business. Some of them, I don't know why they're there."

"John, you have to assess. How else can we know what they need?"

"I know what they need."

"OK, I'll bite, what do they need?"

"I need more of them to be like…" He named his favorite GM.

"What do you like about him? The way he dresses? Makes charts? Plays golf? What?"

"I like that he gets business results. I like that he has credibility in front of the customer. I like that he can put a team together and drive them hard." He took the list of potential GMs, compiled by the business unit HR primes, and said, "I'll do your assessment." He went down the list, writing either "yes" or "no" next to the names, while sometimes adding a real derogatory remark against certain people. "He's lazy. Why's he on the list? This is what you bring me?"

"Well, John, I'm trying to get at some criteria here."

He'd had enough of this conversation. He picked up the phone and called Roger, who was in charge of planning the upcoming GM Forum: "I'm sending Tim to help."

As soon as I could, I called Roger, who said, "I don't need any help. What does John want you to do?"

"I don't know."

"Well, come on down to Dallas."

By the time I got to Dallas, he said, "Eric tells me you're a good guy." I read into that, "So I can trust you." Before that endorsement, he thought I was some HR guy that John's sending in to spy. What people would read into that was, "I must be in trouble."

I didn't do much on that first GM Forum. Roger had it all set. He knew what he was doing. He had top-notch external speakers introduce the concept of Customer Value Management[4]. He also sprinkled in a few internal speakers, highly polished and entertaining. There was no attempt to formally launch the model. At the end of the event, John pulled me aside and said, "I want you to put the next GM Forum together. I want to do it sooner rather than later."

"Fine," I said, "What do you want out of it?"

"I really want to test their business acumen. I don't think they understand that the world of long product development and long product life cycles is over. We have to compete in the data world, which is short/short, not long/long."

---

4 *Managing Customer Value,* by Bradley Gale.

He personally led the development of a set of templates, getting input from his marketing and finance teams. He wanted each GM to get up and talk about their business in terms of these product/market lifecycle charts. "Some of them don't get it. Even some of them who understand their product life cycle don't understand that there's a market lifecycle." As a dinner speaker, we invited Paul Weifells, who had worked on the book, *Inside the Tornado*,[5] as John wanted them to understand the culture of high growth companies.

For the month or so that the GMs were scurrying around filling out their templates, I was concurrently interviewing them, asking them what they felt were the barriers to implementing this model. Most of the stated barriers were about blame. Most of the blaming was on corporate. The barriers were, "I can't get *good* data from Finance." "I can't get *timely* data from Finance." "IT is terrible." "Systems are useless." "We have no processes." "HR is terrible." "Corporate staff has their own agenda." "Corporate is driving John's agenda; they're not working across boundaries. They're not team players."

Before I went to see John, I went to see the people in charge of the things the GMs were complaining about: *all the corporate heads!*

Every one of them wanted a slot at the forum to explain why their corporate group really was meeting the business needs. Things would get better if the GMs would just comply. For example, I met with John's CFO, Frank Dunn. "You know, Tim, I'll show you some stuff." He showed me some chart decks detailing Finance projects, Finance budgets, etc. "We can do anything John wants us to do. We could stop all this other stuff and spend a lot of money and rebuild the Finance system and give them the type of P & L information they want, the type of daily information they want,

---

5 *Inside the Tornado: Strategies for Developing, Leveraging, and Surviving Hypergrowth Markets,*by Geoffrey A. Moore

just like Cisco supposedly does. It would cost us millions of dollars to develop that system, and John says 'no.' So you don't have any beef with me. You have a beef between the GMs and John. Right now John won't invest in us changing Finance's systems."

I went on my little treadmill to John, "If I listen to the corporate people, the whole Forum will be corporate people giving presentations." We both laughed. "You know, having me collect this data, our credibility is at stake. Your credibility; my credibility. We collect data, we learn things, and we don't act on them. When I go out the next time, they're going to tell me to piss off. To a certain extent, they're right. You have not let go."

"Are they crazy? Do they think I can let go? I'm just going to risk the whole company and hold my breath?" He didn't trust them enough to let go. He didn't really trust the GM model implementation strategy. It was taking too long. I think he believed we needed it, but he didn't trust that our capability gap would be closed in time. Most GMs wanted ownership of their own domain, their own "sandbox." It was a "catch 22." You have to change the infrastructure to find out if they were any good or not, but it's expensive and risky so you can't change the infrastructure. "They have to earn it. They have to show me their worth. Besides, I don't have any money. I don't run a business. They're the business leaders. Tell them if they need a new Finance system, they can fund it."

I went back and talked to the small core of GMs that I trusted the most. They went nuts. "Sure, I'll fund it, but they won't build it my way. Frank wants me to come design it? Isn't that Frank's job?" Everyone was on this roundabout of circular logic and finger pointing.

At the second, and unfortunately what would prove to be the last, GM Forum, I thought we would all die of boredom. It was thirty-five presentations on the same templates. In fact, even John's interest started to fade, so the poor people who had to present on day three were victimized. He had lost his patience. Too many of them could not fully satisfy his penchant for detail. There was way too many promising to get back to him. We wound up appeasing the corporate heads and packed several staff presentations into the third day.

I was busiest in the white space, the breaks from the formal parts of the program. People would grab me in the hallway, buy me drinks in the bars, and even track me down in the gym. In fact, the white space was always a frenzy of disjointed activity. Many felt that this was where the real work got done; this networking was the best part of the meeting. "If you're going to bring us together, build more white space. In fact, why don't you bring us together without John? Maybe we can learn from each other because all we want to do here is get through these presentations that John has us doing to get to the bar and get to the meals because that's where we work. We're getting tons of work done by meeting each other."

Many of the private meetings were attempts to subvert the infamous "trading rules." The organization model itself was perceived to be a barrier. In the minds of Nortel executives, there's only one relevant question raised by any organization model: who owns the P & L? If you're not reporting a real P & L, everything else is moot. As a result of my interviews and analysis, John created what were called, informally, "gear box" roles. He took people that he trusted and said, "You're going to be the interface between Europe and product people in North America." When a North American-based business sold into a World Trade division country, the gear boxes had to resolve any internal strife: Who gets revenue and earnings credit? Which sales team gets compensated for what? When multiple products, from different business units, got bundled together as a network, battles ensued to decide which product line got hit with the discount pricing. The gear box roles were to provide the grease to make the model work. They tried to give the market organizations "shadow" P & L's. This could not help but spotlight the weaker managers, and the roles became mired in politics, as they tried to fix the power struggle between product and market. Well, market primes wanted to be GMs now. They knew a shadow P & L from a real one.

In addition to the gearbox role, we tried a more traditional approach: a Networks Proposal Marketing Council (NPM). In the 1995 annual report, CEO Jean Monty unveiled the *World of Networks*. After reading it, I called the chief PR writer and said, "This is the best vision document I've ever seen. This is a brilliant job. Glad you wrote it. I only wish it were real."

Jenny asked me to help make the NPM successful. The chair, and therefore the council, lacked a clear mission. GMs saw the council as a make-work role, assigning people they could *spare*. We could not get people who had responsibility, authority, and credibility assigned.

But the *business problem* was real: we still couldn't effectively take a network offer. It was one of the classic absurdities: we were bragging about our World of Networks, and we didn't have processes to market and sell networks. The council became the place to cobble offers together, rather than to develop protocols and processes. It had been five years since Paul Stern first called us "warring tribes." The skirmishes were still vicious.

Lacking a better strategy, we expanded on the competency model, the interviews, all the data from the GM Forums, and compiled a "General Manager Success Profile." We distributed it to all the GMs and included the business managers so they would know what it takes to get to the next level. We came up with the idea to leverage the HR generalists to help implement the model. I had begun leading a monthly OD call for generalists who wanted to form a community of practice. A lot of these folks were assigned to support GMs. Why not raise their capability, so they could better coach their clients? We designed and delivered a workshop to educate them on the intent of the model and bring them together as a network, both to develop them and strengthen the business. A win-win.

One of the actions out of that workshop was to start the GM Coaches Network. I held calls for the better part of a year, sharing stories and extracting lessons out of the day-to-day business issues. We really tried to raise the bar on the whole coaching process. Too little, too late. The business had stalled, and John began to pull back. He wrote some candid memos that said, in effect, *this model's not going well because I'm not getting the earnings. If you can't be trusted to get me the earnings, then how can I give you more accountability and responsibility? If you don't get the earnings soon, we're going to revert to the corporate control model!* Painfully close to the old HR saw, "The beatings will continue until morale improves!"

We tried to keep the model alive, held "mini" GM Forums, but these were merely glorified business operations reviews. We never really got the chance to escalate the GM *development*. "Develop on what?" I kept asking. I tried to get a critical mass of volunteers to pilot the assessment tool, but the GMs were afraid. A few of them asked me, "What happens if I don't measure up?" I promised safeguards, at the same time worrying that I would not be able to deliver them.

Perhaps the most frustrating aspect for me was that I only got lip service from my fellow HR execs, and I began to wonder if there

was something in the HR culture that resisted leadership development. I sometimes saw HR execs like the guys in the circus that follow the elephants around. Wear a suit that blends in, stay out of the
light, but clean up the shit. I imagined that strong leaders wouldn't
need so many HR people looking after them. Furthermore, having
measurable criteria and building the ability to assess and develop
them might take subjective HR out of the loop in personnel decisions. That responsibility was a significant source of our power.
I accused several business unit HR VPs, "You don't really want a
leadership system, because it takes the power away from you!"

Only one of them admitted, solemnly, privately, "Yeah, we like
that power."

CHAPTER 11

CUSTOMER FIRST

It started with a cold call from Adrian, a vice-president in Marketing: "I'm chairing a new council for Jean [Monty, the new CEO] called Customer First (CFC). I want you to do one of those Future Search things for me."

"Before I agree to that, I need to understand the council's purpose. What are you trying to do? What are the expected outcomes?"

We had a few conversations. To my ear, he described a disparate group of people forced to come together in search of a mission. When I asked him who the client was, he answered, "the business." Always a red flag. It may be that the value created would improve the business, but clients had to be people. He would have to enroll the product presidents as stakeholders.

Adrian had seen the outcome of a Future Search process I had facilitated, which resulted in a new Integrated Marketing Communications function. Although flattered that he thought the work was significant and had impact, I did not want to be a solution in search of a problem. The essence of Future Search is getting the "entire system" in the room. He didn't have a system yet. There was no team, no organization. All of my successes with the Future Search methodology had been with intact organizations. "I really don't think it's going to be productive to take the council offsite and try to do a Future Search. In fact, I don't think I can help you from the outside. I think in order to help you I need to be on the inside, become part of the group." He had me appointed to the council, and I began to facilitate their meetings as a member of the team.

Paul Stern had successfully described the "warring tribes" syndrome that had internal groups competing for the customers' attention and dollars, but he had been unable to make a lot of progress in addressing the underlying culture that drove these behaviors. He had run a rah-rah Excellence! program as a whistle-stop political campaign, complete with bus, bunting, and buttons. Concurrently, he was firing people for noncompliance and establishing a forced ranking system, intending to shed the bottom tier of poor performers. He was obsessed with cost reduction and gutted the R+D budget, alienating customers who started to bail in droves. His slogan, V2K, Vision 2000, was all about numbers, absent a strategy of how to achieve them. Focusing mostly on short-term profits, he was unable to sustain the board's support. His departure had come swiftly.

The board reached back into Bell Canada to anoint Jean, who declared his mission to reconnect to the customer. The international Quality movement had established the axiom that you can only get the change you want by measuring for it. Metrics drive results. The Customer First Council would be his vehicle to improve the capability to measure. Adrian had been influenced by the customer value management approach that Bradley Gale had promulgated at the first general manager forum, and he wanted to leverage the council to bring that level of focus to the company. He had secured representatives from each of the major businesses and they had been meeting for a few months before he called me.

He had also hired an external consultant, Ray Kordupleski. Ray had done customer satisfaction for AT&T for twenty-eight years before setting up as an independent. Ray brought experience, expertise, research, and data. His discipline produced reams of statistics, tables, and formulas. He emphasized the concepts of "relative customer value" and "customer loyalty." Loyal customers are the ones who buy repeatedly and who will refer you to other customers. Repeat orders drive profitable growth. If your value is perceived to be higher, *relative to your competitors,* loyalty escalates. Ray shared the science to measure it[1].

The first meeting I facilitated was in Dallas. To me, Adrian's introduction felt like, "There's a new guy on the team, and by the way he's from HR, and he's going to help us become a stronger team." I got the looks from the line guys right away. The first day, their regular agenda was mind numbing. It was technical presentation after technical presentation. Every business prime got up and presented statistical charts, formula charts, and lots and lots of numbers. Ray and Adrian were making most of the observations. My guess was that the line guys did not want to criticize each other.

During the coffee and lunch breaks, I overheard some of the "Customer Satisfaction Primes" worrying about whether their role was legitimate or not. Some of them had been appointed because of their affiliation with Quality. To the line execs, this customer sat stuff looked like quality stuff. Too often, corporate-driven change efforts were routinely delegated to staff groups, so they gave the responsibility for this one to Quality. Even the corporate quality prime was there and, in fact, there was a lot of deference to him, especially by the people who used to dotted-line report to him.

There were an awful lot of "dead horses" lying around this council, but everyone was walking gingerly around them, pretending they weren't there, even as they began to rot and smell. At the end of a brutal day, we all went to dinner and had a couple of drinks. The astute lobbyists were schmoozing, trying to find out what my real agenda might be.

In true NTL fashion, reacting to what the people in the room needed, I designed my gig for the second day about one o'clock in the morning. Drawing on a Future Search module, I opened the meeting by gathering a timeline of "prouds" and "sorries." I went around the room, asking each participant to tell stories about the things that made them the most proud, or the sorriest, related to

---

1 *Mastering Customer Value Management,* Ray Kordupleski and Janice Simpson.

customers. I needed a little understanding of the history of these people and this effort, to see where the common ground might be. This approach always stimulated reflective conversations. I thought it would take an hour or so, but it took the better part of the morning.

Several people listed their experience with the Excellence! program as their "proud" and several people listed their experience with the Excellence! program as their "sorry." The ensuing conversation was deferential; some folks were walking on eggshells because the corporate guy who had run the program was in the room. After a while of careful listening, he stepped up and said, "You know, let's cut through some BS here, OK? I have 'sorries' about Excellence! You're not hurting my feelings by talking about Excellence! In fact, let's talk about Excellence! because we screwed it up. We turned it into a 'program.' I let that happen."

I reset the environment to capture this insight, moving tables out of the way and putting the chairs in a big circle. Courageously, he poured his heart out for thirty minutes about his learnings from Excellence! I took note of how enthralled, almost reverent, everyone was. Out of that I was able to spotlight the fear that these people had that Customer First was "just another program," implying that it would be treated like a corporate program and would be measured like a corporate program. Therefore, they would become corporate program geeks.

Adrian validated that these fears were legitimate and that he was not immune. He said, "You know, I left a business role. I have no desire to become a corporate program geek. But, you know, Jean asked for our help. Can we not rally around 'maybe it's good for the customer'? And maybe it's going to be good for the company for us to work together as if we were a team and not let it become a corporate program?"

After a day filled with honest and heartfelt dialogue, I debriefed Adrian: "Your leadership was spot-on. You have their attention and you have their respect. But, you don't have a team, in any way, shape or form. You don't have shared objectives; you don't have shared accountabilities. You're a working group[2]. Right now you're just a bunch of people who get together to compare notes. There's a lot of fear, and I don't think you have anything to offer them other than a corporate program. You're well down the path to becoming a corporate program. The tokens are there. The symbols are there."

"Just help me figure out what to do next."

Despite the fears, I was impressed at how much talent was on the council. My design for the next meeting backfired a bit. I had said, "Let's talk about who you are as a member of this group." I intended to surface the rest of the fears and begin to get at some of the hopes and aspirations, all the time getting a handle on the true level of commitment. Instead, I enabled each member to bring his or her "pet rocks" into the room. Each brought his or her favorite solution. Everyone was talking about the databases they use to put their customer sat numbers in, and they wound up arguing about whether we should be using a five-point or a seven-point Likert scale. There was too much personal stuff and chest thumping. It was a challenge to pull common ground out of that mess. It was much easier to represent a flavor-of-the-month solution than it was to fully articulate the business issues that we were trying to resolve. I squeezed them about whether they had any authority or influence back into their businesses. Some of them were three layers down from the president and e-mailed in a monthly report.

We actually came out of that meeting with an agreed-to contract as to how we were going to get common business rules and processes to drive improvement. I would later learn that some of them were passive aggressive. On points that they didn't win, they

---

2 *The Wisdom of Teams,* Jon R. Katzenbach and Douglas K. Smith

never actually changed their process, even though they had *agreed to change*. As part of my effort, I went to see each product president. More than one told me that the CFC was a distraction. "I'm only letting my guy go to the meetings because I don't want the noise. I don't need Jean calling me asking why I'm not being a 'team player.' But I know what I'm doing with customers. I don't need a corporate council to tell me how to treat my customers."

After three or four months, some relationships started to solidify. We started to get "beyond the data." I got them to agree to stop reviewing each other's reports in the meetings. They shared that data offline. Instead of presenting numbers charts, we started to have conversations about what the data said.

The interesting patterns that started to emerge out of the data were that customers really liked Nortel employees and they liked the relationship with Nortel. But over all they thought Nortel processes were broken. They would become very frustrated because they would hear from both their sales relationships and the technical support groups that Nortel was broken internally, saying, "I'll do what I can for you, but I don't know if I can fix it, because *they* don't care." *They*, of course, being other Nortel groups. Jonathon Calof[3] would later describe a "black cloud" forming over the customers, a metaphor for the erosion of trust, as a major reason the company eventually failed. In hindsight, I can see the seeds of the cloud being sown by our front line employees.

There was a lot of evidence that a lot of front line employees were clueless about how to get systemic change, systemic fixes. This confused the customer as it did two things simultaneously: it endeared certain individuals to the customers because they could say, "I care about you. I'll do whatever I can. I'll even break processes; I'll break the rules. I'll even carry purloined spare parts around in the trunk of my car if I have to. I can't get you all your parts at once because they're so stupid back there in manufacturing." But the accumulation of this behavior was actually poisoning

---

3   *An Overview of the Demise of Nortel Networks*, University of Ottawa, 2014.

the customer relationship, as customers worried about relying long-term on a supplier whose employees constantly complained about their bosses, their processes and their company. Meanwhile, loyalty wasn't breeding.

We had this big aha moment that the processes were broken; the people were fine. We would have to do some frame-breaking things in order to fix the processes, which cross businesses and functions. The primes wanted to turn to corporate to accomplish this paradigm shift. They thought I should have enough perspective to *tell* the presidents how to fix things. "Oh, no," I said. "You're the ones who don't want this to become a corporate program. You're the ones in the lines of business. Fix the business processes from within; do not expect outsiders to do it for you."

In fact, though, another corporate group, Business Process Support Services (BPSS), had begun operating under an entrepreneurial business model, offering to work on processes for those businesses that could afford to pay for their services. The group did some important work, for a while, at least until money became tight. Then it was choked to extinction.

The Customer First intervention reached its first anniversary. "I'm with you guys for a year now. In the beginning, we talked about getting shared objectives, shared accountabilities. We made some progress toward that. And yet each of you is still doing your own thing."

We never coalesced into a real team. But we did have a lot to show. We produced a document called the "Customer First Roadmap." When you look at the depth of the content, it's brilliant. It's perfect. It's beautiful. It says measure correctly, measure the right stuff for the right reasons, and then put plans together to fix the right stuff. A few of the businesses began implementing fully and achieved vastly improved customer satisfaction scores. Simple and self-evident, but company-wide institutionalization would prove elusive. Fixes required cross-functional, cross-business teamwork. There was no true corporate mandate to follow the roadmap.

For me, a pattern was emerging. I learned that people really don't mind change, but they do mind *being changed*. The same principle applies to organizations. Executives get to the top, in part, due to their ability to make decisions. They like the power that comes with that capability and they like to control their own organizations. Corporate, in its attempt to look across organizations, comes across as a barrier, an important one, not to be ignored, but a barrier nonetheless. At its worst, corporate presents as a disease, spreading "programitis." The dreaded cliché, "I'm from corporate, and I'm here to help," was too oft heard as a parody.

Having said that, change efforts disturb the system, and validating the rules of chaos theory[4], once disturbed the system will never be the same. The CFC raised awareness and built capability. Upon the council's recommendation, Jean added customer satisfaction metrics to the executive compensation bonus structure. Astoundingly, it helped raise the company's CSAT from a mediocre 65 percent to a world-class 89 percent, and each and every member of the council deserved part of the credit. The long-term success of a corporate program is that when the program dissipates, the intentions continue without policing. Success means that the learning has taken place that helped institutionalize some new behaviors. Individual businesses carried on many of the efforts, evidence that Customer First was a definite success.

---

4 *Leadership and the New Science*, Margaret Wheatley.

CHAPTER 12

"I WANT TO CHANGE THE CULTURE"

As the corporate VP of OD, I was supposed to coach each of the business unit HR vice-presidents. A true action-learning experiment: I was to work on strategic business issues *with* the HR VPs for *their* clients, and through the work, build the OD capability of the HR leaders. As an individual contributor, all of my value would be delivered through personal influence. I had no authority and no staff. Jenny suggested I start with the Broadband business and first schedule some time with Ian Craig, the president. "OK," I said. "To do what?"

"I don't want to bias you before you begin. Just go talk to him."

In his landmark book, *Flawless Consulting*, Peter Block advises, "Authentic behavior with a client means that you put into words what you are experiencing with the client as you work."[1] This is especially true at the beginning of the relationship, when the consultant, or coach, enters the system. Making entry into an OD intervention is not always as formal as it was with Customer First, sometimes only recognized through hindsight.

---

1 *Flawless Consulting*, p. 37.

Authenticity, as Block goes on to point out, is necessary to build a real trust relationship. In my first meeting with Ian, it was easy for me to be authentic, as I had nothing to sell, nothing to push, no pet rocks to protect. Ian talked about how broadband technology would create new markets for our transmission equipment. Deregulation accelerated the creation of new markets and new customers. He was also wondering what the impact of all this might be on our traditional customers. Toward the end of our conversation, I said, "Let me come to your meetings and hang out." At this stage it was a weak contract, but one that we agreed to.

During this period of making entry, I was talking with Ian's HR VP, Caroline, every day. I knew my job could only be viable with her as an advocate. We treated each other as partners. She trusted that I wouldn't try to usurp her position. I was not interested in eroding or siphoning any of her power.

As I attended the first few cabinet meetings, I was very careful about what I said, listening intently and asking salient questions, knowing that I had to gain credibility and trust with this team before I could influence them. About three months into it, at a late night bar session after a staff meeting, Ian cornered me and said, "I want a completely different culture for Broadband Networks."

"Why?"

He started listing all the things that were wrong with Nortel's current culture: too internally competitive, too technology focused, and not enough customer focus. There wasn't enough trust. I kept peeling the onion with him and asking him why he wanted a different culture. At the end of the conversation, I said, "No."

He was taken aback. "What do you mean, no?"

"All you did was list negatives about Nortel. You haven't mentioned why this would be good for the customer or how it's going to help the business. Think about that and let's talk again next month."

A reinforcing reason for saying no was my agenda about leadership. I believed Ian was a model of the new kind of leader that

Nortel needed. A deeply intelligent Scotsman, he used literary references, often quoting Robert Burns, the genius poet and lyricist, the famous Scot who wrote "Auld Lang Syne." Ian shared his humor and wit. He was a sincere and authentic listener. He had demonstrated that he was a lifelong learner, quite comfortable in his own skin. I envisioned Ian as the voice of a new model of leadership, so that when his business succeeded, the company would notice that there *was* something important about this new leadership system.

I had read enough about Appreciative Inquiry[2] to know that if Ian tried to change the culture because it was broken, it would just be business-as-usual—one executive carping about his peers—and doomed from the start. The energy it would take to alter Nortel's culture would only come by inspiring people to be part of something great. Creating something generates its own momentum. Fixing things requires constant application of force. I was absolutely clear about the importance of that first "no."

The next time I asked Ian "why," he led with, "Our customers will demand it because *they* have different cultures. Nortel's culture mirrors our customers' cultures. The RBOCs have a three-year capital expense cycle, so we built around that. They were content to wait *years* for product development. They have always wanted long-term deals. We make the deals on the golf course and work out the details later. But this isn't how it works with the start-ups. It isn't how it works in the data world. They want new products in *months*."

I launched into a spiel that I had been mentally devising. "Culture is a collection of behaviors. We behave based on our beliefs and assumptions. If you hope to change other people's beliefs and assumptions, you have to be clear about your own. First, we

---

2 Appreciative Inquiry is a particular way of asking questions and envisioning a future that fosters positive relationships and builds on the basic goodness in a person, a situation, or an organization. In so doing, it enhances a system's capacity for collaboration and change. *The Power of Appreciative Inquiry* defines AI as "the study and exploration of what gives life to human systems, at their best."

start with who you are, and then build self-awareness of the individuals on your cabinet. Then we mold them into a team." I laid out an approach for building a plan. He agreed with the reasoning, and so it began.

Driving change, overcoming resistance from multiple sources, requires tremendous courage and a lot of energy and stamina. The results from the changes may be unpredictable. Dealing rapidly and honestly with unintended consequences builds credibility and sustains momentum. Ian would have to be self-confident to the point of admitting when he was wrong and adapting on the fly. Resisters will barrage with questions, undermine, and even sabotage the effort. The leader can have doubts about what he is doing, but not doubts about who he is, or why he is doing it. If he had these self-doubts, the resisters would chip away at his resolve and he would grow unsure, losing his ability to drive the change. Establishing that he valued self-awareness, welcomed and even embraced feedback, learned from his mistakes and still went forward enabled him to be heard, to be respected, admired, and even loved.

The first step was to figure out how to get the work done, since I had no staff. The project had to be run from within Ian's business, and owned by Ian's cabinet. My role would be mostly sideline coaching—to Ian, Caroline, some of her staff and other cabinet members—and some group facilitation.

In terms of content, we used many of the assessment tools from the Center for Creative Leadership. In order to grow as a team, to trust each other and improve their business model, the cabinet members had to make a dramatic commitment, *by their actions*, to learning. Having a president use the tools concurrently with his staff was a first, creating a safe environment for others to learn.

In parallel, we wanted to conduct an organizational assessment so that the cabinet members could understand the status quo and the issues that were most important to the business and the customer. Caroline liked the approach but wouldn't have the time to perform all the detailed work. The HR VP's role was focused on the "darn dailies": organization structure, talent issues, relationship issues, leadership issues and business issues. She assigned Helen, from her staff, as project manager, a developmental assignment to prepare her for promotion. I agreed to coach her, to help her build OD capability. When making the transition from being an operational HR person to working more strategically with executives, she would need to be clear about outcomes and measurements; be flexible about where the group needs to be; be fast on her feet, able to change on a moment's notice; and finally, not hold the client accountable to her agenda.

Caroline retained a key role in helping to shape and facilitate Ian's cabinet meetings, to help me keep the culture change work integrated with the business issues.

Ian had developed a practice of opening each staff meeting with a focus on the customer. "Who's got an order?" he'd ask, and several called out a deal that they had either just closed or were about to close. In the other business units, meetings routinely opened with a presentation by Finance, an internal focus on the numbers, with emphasis on where they were "soft." This served to put the product leaders on the defensive right at the start of the meeting.

Ian's practice, on the other hand, served to start the meeting with an external focus, with a focus on the customer, with a positive focus on the future. There were numerous smiles, a little vying for some of the attention, and a relaxed atmosphere all around. Only after this ritual was completed to his satisfaction did he ask for the agenda to be displayed.

Within hours, though, the meetings looked pretty traditional, the charts predictable, the issues routine. The product owners often blamed their issues on staff: manufacturing was too expensive, service was too thin, and our trading rules with other Nortel businesses were too complex and inhibited our ability to sell networks. I probed for accountability, challenging the mental model that it was OK to blame others. My interventions were subtle and slight, calculated to affect their thinking. Out of the corner of my eye, I caught Ian's twinkling smile.

Early on, I detected some fear, especially as the cabinet members started to learn that Ian would be sharing his 360-degree feedback results with the whole team. At one end of the continuum, people were telling me how much they supported the work and what their concerns were. At the other end of the scale, some were asking me, "What the hell are you doing. Ian is our boss; we have to have faith in him. We do not want to know his faults!" Most startling was their overall lack of self-esteem and confidence. These were top, successful executives. Filled with insecurities and uncertainties, they wanted reassurance from a relatively new—to them—staff guy.

Even so, the hallway conversations, the impromptu phone calls, and the cryptic e-mails helped build my confidence: they were going to include me in their thinking; they were going to take the risk and trust, or pretend to trust, me.

Caroline invited me to their GM Reflection Sessions. These were satellite events, held over dinner before the regular business meetings. Ian threw out a topic like, "Where do you think the CLEC market will be in five years?" These were long-term business strategy topics. Soft topics, like career development, never fit. The conversations were freewheeling and covered a lot of territory.

She had picked up the idea from a short monograph by Charles Handy, *Managing the Dream: The Learning Organization*. The idea was that the learning process is a wheel. It begins with *questions*, which can be triggered by problems or issues. These questions demand solutions that demand *ideas*. Implementations of these ideas are called *tests* until proven. The results of the tests are studied as *reflections*. Ideally, the wheel spins continuously. It seemed obvious to us that Nortel usually skipped the reflection piece, moving rapidly through the other quadrants, but rarely stopping to learn. After one of these stimulating evenings, a senior GM told me, "This's the most important thing we do when we get together."

"Why?"

"Because we're looking into the future. We're putting strategy together, we're customer-focused and we're not basing any of it on today's stock price, *and* we're bonding as a team. We're getting to know each other at a pretty deep level."

As usual, the spectrum was broad. Another member told me that these same dialogues were a waste of time: "We're not addressing today's issues."

"Thanks for sharing," my standard response to the whiners. "Why don't you share that with Ian or with the group tonight and see what they think? Either go public with your views, or relax and trust the process." This pattern of wanting to use HR to carry bad news to the boss was deeply engrained in the culture. This was a typical example of the seduction of being perceived as a business confidante, someone with indirect power who can pull strings behind the scenes. In this case, my sense of the new leadership model I was envisioning didn't have a place for the "tell it to HR" game. I wanted these guys to start telling the truth *to each other.*

Ian decided to further change the format of his business meetings. He said, "You know, we get together, we spend all this time and money, flying people in from all over, and then we do routine stuff. The reality is I'm trying to build a future; I'm trying to build a strategy. We tack that on to an ops review and maybe we get to it and maybe we don't. So I want to make that primary."

Ian was really paying attention to behavior, including his own. He became aware that people were bringing him decisions that they had the capabilities and the authority to make, and then they got upset with him because *he* wouldn't make them. His team was still expecting the dominance model of leadership and he had moved beyond it. Through a series of conversations, he arrived at the decision of doing the ops review virtually, by phone. He reasoned, "Let's morph the ops reviews from looking at everything to looking only at those things we need to look at. What if we have my CFO hold a conference call with all the GMs and look at their numbers? Then he can tell me which one or two businesses we need to worry about, rather than have everybody come with the same set of charts to show me that their numbers are on track or a little behind or a little ahead. Let's have him do that. If he identifies one that is worthy of our focus, let's not dwell on why the numbers are bad; let's dwell on how to make the numbers good. Let's not look backward and try to blame anyone. Let's look forward and see how we grow this business."

Changing the nature of the business meeting was heretical. They were the most holy, most sacred rituals: the central demonstration that the heads of the hierarchy held the business together. They struck fear into the hearts of most presenters. The divisional leaders presented the status of their P+L's. We would analyze and discuss the numbers from the development cycle thru the product introduction and product maturity cycles. Deep, detailed piles of data on revenues, earnings, expenses, margins, on and on, were presented product-by-product, market-by-market in hushed and serious tones.

Over the years, the objective became to present better than your peers, no matter how bad your numbers might look. Although the entire top management team would sit in the same room for ten-, twelve-, or fourteen-hour days, the meeting would be a series of successive presentations to the president and his CFO. Gamesmanship and creative chart production were distinctive capabilities. Exploiting your knowledge of technology might hide your ignorance of business. There was very little critiquing of each other. Each presenter would be afraid to say anything about anyone else's charts for fear of retaliation when they got up themselves. "Getting shot," was the biggest fear of all: "I'm going to get shot when I present these numbers."

Fear rolled downhill and infused the work environment for weeks before each meeting. At every level, groups of people focused on making PowerPoint charts—remaking them after dry-runs and remaking them again and again to please the latest whim of the boss. Some would spread their charts out on a conference table and agonize over each word, each nuance. Too often, many of these charts were never shown. The first presenters in the morning would get the most attention. Agendas would often be hours late before noon. Promises were made and actions recorded. Then the boss flew out of town, on to the next site.

Changing the very nature and process of the ops reviews turned out to be akin to altering DNA with herbal tea. It was a great, tasty experiment, but would prove to be of limited success. We began by inviting Stan Gryskiewicz from the Center for Creative Leadership. He had been working on a concept he called "Positive Turbulence," which he would later capture in a book by the same name. The idea is to look just outside your accustomed periphery. Read things you don't normally read and go to conferences just outside your usual boundary. New inputs will help you disturb your belief system and create new ideas. He introduced us to new magazines, like *Wired*, *Red Herring*, and *Fast Company*.

We brought in a succession of speakers to create positive turbulence. For example, Martha Rogers came in to speak about her book, *The One to One Future*. Our intention was to focus more on customers and their unique needs, to impede the loss of market share to start-ups. During the presentation, Martha made it a point to relate to our lone female line executive, making a lot of eye contact and giving examples like, "Wouldn't you like it if your jean size was measured, and you could order your jeans and they'd be shipped to you and you wouldn't have to go to GAP and find that you're in between sizes?" Then she went into a whole riff around bras. "You know, some of us have one breast smaller than the other. And sizes don't deal with that. Wouldn't it be nice to get a bra that fits you?"

After the meeting a lot of the guys were angry, saying that it was inappropriate for a woman to come in and talk about bras and breast sizes. We had created turbulence, but it wasn't positive. One of them even asked me, "Couldn't I consider this sexual harassment? I was very uncomfortable." He had missed the whole point of the one-to-one marketing part of Martha's message.

Ingar Skaug, CEO of Wilhelmsen Lines from Norway, was invited to another meeting. He told his captivating story about coming to the helm after an absolute catastrophe: the entire leadership team of the company had been killed in an airplane crash. While talking about how he changed the culture of the company, the conversation took an interesting turn. The cabinet wanted to know, "How do we do what Ingar did? How do we follow the formula that Ingar followed?"

I started to worry about the pattern of them delegating their own thinking to these outside experts. In his book, *The Deep Blue Sea,* CCL's Wilfred Drath identifies three tasks of leadership: set an objective, motivate the people, and adapt to change. Our cabinet didn't get that what Ingar was good at was *adapting to change.* They wanted some *formula* about how to set the objectives and motivate the people.

Finally, another speaker was David Hurst, author of *Crisis and Renewal,* in which he compares corporate lifecycles to ecosystems. He had done his homework, reading thirty-five years of Nortel's annual reports. He mapped how Nortel history compared to his research models. His model positioned us for a rebirth, which we probably experienced in 1995–96. He prophetically highlighted that his model predicted we would probably burn out and collapse in 2000 if we did not do something to alter our environment!

The cabinet was trying to learn and listen and adapt the learning, but our approach let them off the hook. They were avoiding the deep processing that change demanded. Positive turbulence is supposed to *influence* your thinking, not *direct* your thinking. The cabinet seemed to *react* to the speakers rather than *reflect.* For example, their action item out of Martha's session: "We want to be one-to-one marketing; we get it now." Each speaker provided some nugget that became an icon, a patchwork quilt of ideas looking for a center. They were looking for external answers because there was this internal void. On the other hand, I was personally enthralled at the learning and creativity that *was* going on, at the level of experimentation, at the courage I was seeing. This was much better than ops reviews!

Privately, Ian expressed some self-doubt that he didn't show others, a lot of concern that the larger system would reject this approach. It was late at night during an offsite, and we were well into a bottle of port. I smiled tightly, "We can't sell this as an *idea*. Make Broadband the best business unit in the company. You don't need permission to do these experiments. You only need to deliver results."

About eighteen months into the initiative, the business was on track, growing rapidly. It demanded a lot of attention. Meetings were productive and engaging. The positive turbulence, the external speakers, the leadership development focus—a lot of the interventions that had seemed so innovative less than two years ago—had started to look like business as usual. It had become harder to affect the cabinet members, harder to get them out of their comfort zones. They *expected* to be affected, were ready for changes, and therefore were not as impacted as much.

They also knew that a lot of their markets were maturing and to continue the pace of growth they would have to make new markets, a capability not yet mastered. New products and new technology seemed to come a lot easier than new markets. Several of them asked me, "What now?"

The next cabinet meeting was to be in Park City, Utah. We had reserved a quaint inn during the off-season and would be just about the only guests there. Caroline called me, saying, "Let's do something really different." We tried two new things at this meeting: One worked like a charm, and one worked in ways we never expected.

The thing that worked well was a new approach to getting performance feedback. We videotaped the meeting for the first day. CCL's Robert Burnside, who had become an important and valuable partner in our culture change efforts, designed this intervention. Ian and Caroline orchestrated the agenda so that the easier items would be at the beginning of the day and the more difficult ones in the afternoon. Robert and I set up on the periphery, just away from the conference room table. As he ran the camera, we both watched a monitor with a tape-counter on it. If we saw a behavior of interest, we would note the number. Sure enough, as the taping began, a couple of the cabinet members were looking at the camera. The ones who always hated the new stuff glared at me. I tried not to look in their eyes. A couple of others were leaning toward the camera, performing self-consciously for the first hour or two. But by the afternoon, they forgot about the tape being there and got deep into their business issues.

At one point someone was trying to tell Ian something important and he turned it into a joke, dismissing it. As Ian turned away, the speaker's body language was pretty loud, saying, "I'm worried here and you turned it into a joke and blew me off." At the end of the day, Robert and I compared our lists of counter numbers. We knew that out of a ten-hour business meeting we'd only be able to show them five or ten minutes of tape. We chose a few samples that we had both noted.

We had scheduled two hours to dialogue team behavior to start the second morning. It went for four. Robert had provided them some content about the DIM model of leadership as context for the team behavior dialogue. Robert kicked it off, "Tim and I worked to pick out some taped segments. Not too many. Just a few. We're going to show you one at a time. We're showing you things we think you might find interesting." He ran the tape highlighting

Ian's dismissal. Ian sat back in his chair, smiled and said to the aggrieved party, "*Wow*, I really stuck it to you, didn't I?" He went on and on: "Holy cow did I ever stick it to you. Do I do that all the time?" Nonplussed, he was amazed at what he had done, and sorry that he had done it. He modeled perfect behavior about how to look at this kind of data. That night, even the naysayers gave me feedback that the exercise had been one of the most powerful things they had ever done.

The key was that we had built some trust. We had seen many executives look at 360-degree feedback reports and immediately start in with the excuses. "Oh, I know who rated me this way, and she is just upset that she did not get that promotion." They do this all the time. It is a potent defense mechanism. This video, on the other hand, was *their* data. It was not someone else's opinion of their data. The results could not be rationalized away. They could not be denied. This session demonstrated just how different, and difficult, it is to practice the relational dialogue necessary to make meaning as a team.

The second thing we tried also impacted them, but not in the way we hoped. After dinner on the first day, Robert asked each of the cabinet members to write a fable, a metaphor about something that would demonstrate their values. It had to be fiction. It was supposed to be in third person. There wasn't supposed to be any "I." The story was supposed to illustrate, metaphorically, who they were as a member of the team. If you want to be a good team member, you have to let people know who you are. This exercise was to have been a way to self-disclose in a safe manner.

Each had to find a quiet place to write, somewhere private in the inn. We gave them a half-hour to write their stories. Most took almost an hour and were still not finished but we rounded them up and reconvened as a whole group in a comfortable area with soft seating and soft lighting. They read the stories to each other. The drinks were delayed, prompting some whining. It was late at night. These folks were tired and vulnerable.

Ian, of course, went first and told a very creative, witty story about a dragon slayer. The impact of each story was powerful. There were misty eyes. The cumulative effect was almost daunting. Reflection seemed unavoidable. Even so, some couldn't really accomplish the task as assigned. A few couldn't do fiction. A few couldn't do third person. One wrote a story about a real event in his childhood that was heartbreaking. He tried to cover it up, by changing the pronoun as he read the story: "Oh, I mean 'he.'" Only about half of the group was absolutely true to the task. The same people who were troubled by the things we'd been doing all along, the ones who had been most resistant to all the efforts to raise self-awareness, who were resisting the open culture, struggled through this intervention. When everyone was done, Robert simply said, "Goodnight."

I had an encounter one time with a middle manager who told me, "Tim, you know what your value is? You hold up a mirror to us and you make us look at it. My question to you is, do you always have to stick the mirror right in front of our faces, so we get this big broad view, this magnified look at our warts and blemishes? Can't you hold the mirror to the side every now and then and let us look askance at who we are? Do you always have to shove the mirror right in our faces?" That was pretty interesting feedback. I think that's what was happening here. Some just didn't seem comfortable exposing parts of who they were. It could be that in any group of executives there's going to be that bell curve of people who aren't able or willing to look at that mirror.

Unfortunately, this offsite ended abruptly. Ian was notified about an outage and had to fly to the customer site. Instead of continuing without him, all of the other executives hit the phones and changed their flights, leaving a day early. After bidding farewell to all the clients, Robert and I contracted to take an hour break and then meet for dinner. I drifted out to hike. Unbeknownst to me, Robert climbed the same mountain, from the other side. We met at the summit. We silently watched deer and elk, strolled down the mountain together and walked into Park City for burgers and beer. We returned to the deserted inn talking about Alfred Hitchcock's Bates Motel from *Psycho*. I felt betrayed that the clients had all left. The patriarchy seemed alive and well. If they had stayed for more relational dialogue, I would have felt that all our efforts were really taking root, that shared leadership was starting to be possible. Instead, I drifted off to sleep thinking, "This is not taking."

After Park City, we realized that we had to drive the change deeper into the organization if it was going to gain momentum. We wanted to engage the next few layers of management. They were closer to the edge, closer to the action. They would be in a position to help the cabinet capitalize on the emerging trends and changes in the market place that the cabinet couldn't see. We held a management conference for three hundred business leaders, from all over the world. We hoped to create an environment in which the participants could discover that this new model of leadership was taking hold. Caroline asked me what I thought would be the biggest experiment we could do. "That's easy," I said, "Open Space."

In his book, *Open Space Technology*, Harrison Owen describes it as a self-managed approach to human communication. It starts with a circle of self-selected participants, a few simple rules, and a skilled facilitator. The participants develop the agenda on the spot. People attend whichever breakout sessions they are most drawn to, and are free to leave whenever they choose. Conversations tend to be deep and lively, much like the real work that happens in the white spaces of a formal meeting. Experiences with groups of all sizes have shown it to be a way to get a great deal of business done in a remarkably short time, to make connections and progress in complex situations. Open Space immediately addresses the so-called dead horses in the room as the first order of business. I was drawn to Open Space because I had so often seen that in tightly orchestrated, agenda-bound meetings, the real issues might never come up. Communication stays at the surface and life goes on as usual after the meeting. I thought I could get Harrison, the originator of Open Space, to facilitate.

But, the cabinet asked, "How do you *control* what's going on? How do you know what the decisions will be?" They rejected the idea and planned a more traditional management conference. I was struck by the irony. We were driving down into the organization the concept that management was empowered, yet we orchestrated in advance what the six topics they should pursue would be and who the team leaders should be.

Ian allowed his own traditional core competencies to take over. His energy level was always highest, and he was personally most creative over the years, when he was leading sales conferences. At a retirement dinner for a long-time friend and associate, Ian had corporate communications put together a video concatenation of all the times that he and Ian had been part of outrageous skits at sales conferences. They had imitated everything from talk show hosts to airline pilots, always very splashy, very creative, and very silly: lots of fun, lots of laughs.

Ian ran this gathering like a sales conference. He came up with a new slogan—"Xtreme Networks"—to capitalize on the Xtreme Games that ESPN had just introduced. A group of Gen X professionals wowed the crowd with bicycle stunts, ending with Ian making a grand entrance as someone who had just crashed and mangled his bike. He came onto the stage in a cloud of smoke, carrying a bent frame and wearing a torn leather jacket and a disheveled helmet. The crowd roared as he revealed himself by taking the helmet off. He introduced the Golden Spike award, given in honor of someone for nailing a big order. He gave away all kinds of branded mementos, from jackets to shirts, caps to desk art.

The breakout teams worked feverishly to come up with entertaining skits to illustrate the outcomes of their assigned topics. The themes across the skits were similar. It was clear that people were aligned in terms of what was needed to capture some of the opportunity in the emergent market place. They created the President's Leadership Council, a cross-level, cross-functional advisory council of key resources, just as planned. But it was at this point that I started to get cynical because it was too highly orchestrated. They got what they needed, but this was faux empowerment.

Ian had fun, unaware that he was slipping *my* agenda, reverting to old form, to the things, of course, that had made him successful. I had breakfast with him the last morning and tried to give him this perspective but he was not receptive to it. This conference was a big meeting, with lots of corporate, sales and even other business unit representatives. What he did here was more public. I all but accused him of retreating to his comfort zone to orchestrate a predictable outcome.

On reflection, it may be almost impossible to jump from the dominance model to the making-meaning model. Leaders have to evolve, not transform overnight. The sad part is that maybe the business needed us to leap steps. Again, as a result of deregulation, both the speed of change and the magnitude of change were high, leading to increasingly chaotic conditions. We would have to learn how to adapt quickly as a leadership team. To me, they did not seem ready. They were comfortable and had been very successful in the command and control model. As the business was doing well, I did not have much of an argument to push them harder. I wanted them to soar, but they were content to stand tall.

In reality, Ian was more attuned with his organization than I was. While I wanted him to go faster, many thought he was going way too fast. In terms of readiness across the whole system, the drive for change was mired in the middle, where the P+L metrics kicked in. The front line employees were ready for anything, always anxious to add value and please the customer. But the product line managers were nervous. I began hearing a lot of noise. What if the guys at the top are wrong? Is it safe here? I have an offer from Wireless. Lotta flaky things going on over here. What if Ian misses the market? What if Ian misses the numbers? Wireless is taking a much more careful approach. Should I go to Wireless? What if Broadband has peaked? Isn't Wireless the next new thing? More than once I heard this refrain, attributed to Pogo, the comic strip character: "We have met the enemy, and he is us."

I engaged in a number of very personal conversations. "If you're afraid of risk, you should go to Wireless, if you think it's safer there. If you're driven by fear, then go to Wireless. If you want to be part of something great, or learn a lot even if it fails, then stay in Broadband and see what happens." Anti-cultural advice.

Ian lost some of their trust in this phase, but he didn't know that for a while. The top value at Nortel had always been about delivering results. Some of them questioned whether he still believed that. Of course he did. He believed delivering short-term results, meeting or beating your numbers, needed to be the norm, the expectation, the table stakes. But he also believed another top value for leaders was building the future.

Ian did what he could do in the confines of his complex adaptive system[3] called Broadband Networks. To go further, he needed to influence the encompassing complex adaptive system called Nortel Networks. Ian had been at it for three years, when the reorganization wheel spun again: Ian was announced as chief marketing officer. He lost power because he no longer owned any product lines. Credibility still demanded control of a P&L. He couldn't strongly influence Nortel's culture from the CMO role. I guessed

---

3 Human organizations have been described as networks of humans who interact with each other as individuals. These interactions can provide complex feedback loops that stimulate learning. Such systems can indeed evolve order out of chaos, and even more amazingly, this chaos, or mess, is essential to the process. *Complexity and Creativity in Organizations*, Ralph D. Stacey

that it was a holding pattern, the preannouncement of his retirement, the first phase of a negotiated exit strategy.

We didn't exactly give up, but I felt the larger system, the company as a whole, had barriers to learning. One of the primary barriers was the existing knowledge principle about leadership, what employees really believed about the role of leaders. The dominance principle was the knowledge principle in force. People *expected* their bosses to tell them what to do, to take charge, to take accountability for mistakes and to temper any risks. A common saying was, "What pleases my boss pleases the hell out of me!"

Broadband struggled to learn in this duality. Ian believed in empowerment, trust, and influence—he practiced making meaning and refined the art of relational dialogue. At the same time, his direct reports looked beyond him, into the Nortel Dominance abyss. His influence and behaviors were not spreading beyond the boundaries that he could control. You can't authentically develop leaders pretending that an *influence* principle is the one that's in force, when in reality *dominance* continues to prevail. People quickly sense the façade and get cynical. There's no energy for change in a cynical system.

A dominance-oriented system is all about hero worship, and the compensation system supports individual behavior instead of teams. Thus, you end up with a culture of blame. Dominance as a driving force gets reinforced. If I'm more powerful than you, then I can blame you if things go wrong, and I get more powerful. I win at your expense. The leadership system in place was, in fact, rewarding those who excelled at dominance, even if they exploited the fear to their own advantage. But, the fundamental truth of a hero culture is that if I'm a hero today, it won't be long before I'm a goat. This prevalent fear becomes a powerful engine that drives leaders at all levels.

As you move beyond the dominance knowledge principle, influence and negotiation as knowledge principles require trust and openness to new perspectives. This mode is based on a fundamental respect for the intelligence of others, and a willingness to examine one's own internal dialogue and alter it if new information comes in to challenge it. Therefore, a leader in this mode has to be open to the possibility that s/he doesn't know everything that needs to be known. Dee Hock, in his book *The Chaordic Organization,* says it well: "Current forms of organization are almost universally based on compelled behavior—on tyranny, for that is what compelled behavior is, no matter how benign it may appear or how carefully disguised and exercised." Moving out of tyranny is not a short trip.

Making-meaning is an even longer trip—it's even more incompatible with a hero culture. In a system of leadership formed around making-meaning, no one is a hero, and no one is a goat. Everyone is there to learn, to achieve a shared purpose that emerges from the best aspirations of the people involved. The spiral of increasing empowerment that Ian developed captured the essence of this new leadership model. I amass power for my learning and my knowledge and influence. As soon as I understand it, I give it away. Giving it away gives me the freedom and time to learn new things. So I learn new things, gain new knowledge, get empowered, and then give it away again. Ian had the courage to say, "This making-meaning stuff, this is the real stuff. This is what empowerment is about."

What happens in a Dominance system is an internal dialogue that says, "You're a weak leader because you're giving power away." Ian gave power away. That was pretty flaky. This was absolutely anti-cultural for Nortel. Some saw Ian as a pushover. He was seen by some as weak. A lot of other guys fought for power and left a lot of blood on the table.

Inherent in the Dominance leadership system is that power is the highest reward. Nortel was at a strategic juncture where that system couldn't work. The Dominance system doesn't work where adaptive change is the most important value-added task of leadership. If you're in an environment that's unstable and turbulent, information flow and connectivity are the real sources of power.

The dominant leader can never be smart enough to know it all in a turbulent environment. You have to build a process for leadership because one guy can't do it alone. You have to build a team to get your arms around the complexity enough to be able to make sense of it, choose a response, and implement it fast enough.

Nortel's way of leading was for the top guy to have all the answers, and to reach way down to individual engineers to see what they were doing. Top leaders were the ultimate engineers: clockmakers who designed each detail, puppet masters who pulled a string for each nuance of the organization. Then search for whom to blame when things went wrong.

Ian retired in 2000 with his head held high and the company threw a huge celebration party to thank him for his contribution. After all, his business had won the Triple Crown: Best Customer Satisfaction, Best Employee Satisfaction, and Best Business Results. How much the leadership development work contributed to that success is beyond the capability to measure. For me, I was just sad to see him go, wishing I could find more like him to subvert the dominant paradigm.

I, too, had gone on to a new role, consolidating the company's learning processes. Helen and Caroline kept some of the threads of the intervention alive, working with some of the cabinet members as they went on to new organizations. Toward the end of 2000, actually late one night at La Costa, I shared a drink with two of Ian's disciples, both still successful GMs. Each was stoic, saying, in effect, "We loved the stuff that Ian did; we loved Ian. We still love Ian. It's great stuff. You guys were right. But I can't do it. The system here won't allow it. The company's not ready. I don't have enough energy. I am unwilling to take so much risk." It was a bittersweet moment. As the bar was closing, we shared hugs all around. An unspoken ending.

CHAPTER 13

EMPLOYEE AND ORGANIZATION LEARNING

The analysis from Customer First spotlighted that many of the business processes were mired in self-perpetuation. With extensive growth in the company, many functions had become insular, protecting boundaries, measuring internally and all but ignorant of the impact of their work "downstream," that is, on other organizations that depended on them. All of the issues around business process that I had discovered in NOM were still prevalent years later. I had read many books in trying to discern a new approach to driving change. Through my own path of Positive Turbulence, I happened into the burgeoning literature on knowledge management (KM). KM addressed advanced information management, adaptive change, networked organizations, chaos theory, complex adaptive systems, process reengineering, and, most important, Learning Organizations. Emanating from the seminal ideas of Peter Senge, as described in his book *The Fifth Discipline,* this concept was being promulgated from business magazines and conferences. The argument that complex organizations needed to *learn faster* was patently clear. At this stage, companies that could innovate learning solutions could gain competitive advantage. The evolution of learning processes needed to be pursued with the same rigor that we would put into developing a new product or shaping a new market. I developed an argument that was cogent: the business processes could only be fixed if the employees were empowered, knowledgeable of the "big picture" and secure enough to take risks and tell the truth.

Enrolling Kerry, who relied on her intuition and trust, as a co-conspirator, we devised an approach to talk to the clients in terms they were comfortable with. She led a task force to look at the company's approach to training. We used Jim Pepitone's book, *Future Training*, for inspiration, reducing his thesis to a chart deck, which passed Kerry's "stupid" test: it was simple enough that even busy executives could "get" it at first look. Free of functional jargon, it needed to be business and customer focused. The task force compiled an accounting of the company's total training investment, which topped a hundred million dollars, recommending the creation of a position to work on how we could effectively reduce that amount.

All my experiential learning from NOM, Customer First, GM Model, and Broadband only served to make me an expert on the *problem*: there were too many internal barriers preventing us from putting customer-focused business processes together. These barriers were ingrained in the culture, were long-standing and systemic. They were evident in virtually every HR process, especially promotions, rewards, and compensation. The characterization of the values that we actually *manifested*, rather than *stated*, was easily articulated and universally accepted: we valued heroes over teams, firefighting over prevention, and financial results over value creation. We valued shareholder over customer, never quite believing that the best way to build shareholder wealth would be to truly put the customer first.

Change would have to permeate all layers of the hierarchy, would have to be modeled by leaders throughout the layers and be reinforced by dramatic changes in the HR processes. Only then would the very *idea* of change, the motivation to develop the courage to take risks, be granted an opportunity to germinate. *My* risk, the leap of faith for the company, was that I could leverage my learning and my influence skills to build a team that could craft a solution. Hofmeister had urged us to "embrace ambiguity" and become comfortable traversing "shifting sands." I sensed that chaos and complexity theories would eventually provide the science to confirm his instincts, but I could not yet lay out a detailed plan with predictable and measurable results.

Kerry's corporate Organization Development team helped me simplify the story: We're 80,000 employees; we're at $20B in revenue. The organization structure is very complex, because the value equation to the customer is very complex. It takes a lot of people to produce it. Very large groups of people need to work together, sharing a vision, yes, but sharing objectives and *sharing accountability* for those objectives. Each person needs to feel responsible for the output to the customer, not for pleasing his or her boss. The value-added work gets done through relationships and processes. Fixing those, becoming world-class at those, will bring competitive advantage. Meanwhile, we are spending a hundred million dollars providing training on less important capabilities. Training was the Industrial World's solution to productivity, when performance was predictable and standardizable. Value is created today from innovation. Investing in capabilities like creativity, change management, and teamwork is beyond *training*. Training increased skills in things you already knew how to do. We need to invest in *learning* to beat our competitors at delighting our customers. I believed it in my heart; I embraced it with my soul.

Kerry had the opportunity to take the idea to John's "President's Council." She flew to London, England, to do a thirty-minute presentation recommending the creation of a new executive-level position to focus on learning. She called me from London, immediately after the presentation, saying, "I have good news, and I have bad news."

"OK, what's the good news?"

"They approved the position."

"Give me the bad news."

"They don't necessarily want you in it. They want a slate. And they want you to help with that. Oh, and one other thing, it's going to report to the senior vice-president of HR, not to John." Across the miles, she could feel the emotion rise in my being. "Now, don't get upset," she ordered, "let's just take this one step at a time."

So I wrote a position profile. I was a Band 10 at the time, an assistant vice-president. I wrote the profile for a Band 11, vice-president. I moped through the process of pulling a slate together, positive that I was the best person for this job. I went to the HR VPs to get suggestions and the first round had several expendable staff names, along with a few respected business leaders.

They wanted to make an offer to someone who I felt was not qualified, who was a line Band 10 that they were going to promote to Band 11. They wanted assurance from me that I would work for this person; that I would stay and coach him and be committed to making this program successful. In a very polite way, I articulated the criteria under which I might stay: "If I absolutely and totally respect the person you choose, and that you do not promote a non-qualified person into the role." They made an offer to a line Band 10, one that I respected, but he turned it down. They talked to a few other line leaders. No one wanted it. A few months into this, Kerry called, "They're going to offer you the job. They're going to make it a Band 11. I don't think you should take it."

"Why not?"

"Because of the reporting relationship. You and I designed this to report to the CEO. I don't think you can be successful from HR." Again, the theory being that *staff* could not demand the amount of respect, nor exercise the level of authority that would be needed to drive such a deep change effort. I was being set up for a wealth of passive-aggressive behavior and begrudging compliance. Of course, though, the norm was that a Band 11 would report to a Band 12, not to the CEO. And I was seduced by the allure of being a VP: the perks, the comp, and the stock options!

I stormed into the role, believing my own press, believing that I was going to implement the vision that we had developed. I believed that we were going to figure out how to fix the business processes, flatten the hierarchy, develop the leaders, become world-class in knowledge management, become benchmarkable as a learning organization, delight the customers, beat the competition, win the awards, and solve world hunger!

But it was going to take some time. One of the things I had told Kerry—she threw away the chart long before London—was that culture change was hard; long term systemic change was slow. You need to change people's *behavior, which demands* that you first change their *beliefs*[1]. "We need tremendous leadership and values to drive the change and if we're really good and they're really serious, we can get there in five-to-seven years. This is my last job at Nortel. It's either going to take at least five years and we'll fix the company, or they're not serious and I'll have to quit."

As a first order of business, I flew to Toronto to ask John, "What do you want out of this role?"

"Oh. It's real clear," he said. "It's cost savings." Deja vu?

I said, "OK. But, I also have all this other stuff here." I reviewed the mission of my new organization, Employee and Organization Learning, which was to leverage learning so that we learn faster than our competitors and it gives us competitive advantage. It was a very business-focused mission. We had a broad strategy guideline of three steps: Fix Training; Evolve to Learning; and Build a Framework for Knowledge Management.

"Yes, that's fine. Get me the cost savings and if you get me enough, I'll let you have a little of the money you saved to do your other stuff."

I went back and started the cost reduction work by doing an inventory of training organizations. I hired a terrific CFO who led the team that drove the training cost reduction. In our first year, we took $11 million out of budgets of $62 million. We consolidated organizations from over one hundred to sixty. We pointed to a lot

---

1   For a solid understanding of some of the research, we tried to leverage, see Ken Blanchard's work on *Situational Leadership*, and Nortel's own Tony O'Driscoll's book, *Achieving Desired Business Performance*.

of flaws and a lot of opportunities. When I went to review the results with John, he said, "This is a good start. I want more."

I morphed into Nortel-speak, "To get you more, I have to own
it all, because…" I used the example of the Technology training
department, using it as an example of why I wouldn't be able to
consolidate. "Technology is taking eighty percent of my energy.
It's classic BNR; they absolutely refuse to play. They're on their
own schedule. They're spending more money on training than
anybody else; they're not implementing the new e-learning stuff;
they're not interested in me saying that they could reduce in some
areas. Now if you give it to me, I can *direct* them to do it."

John said, "You might be right."

Weeks went by. A few months went by. I called, saying, "John,
it's not happening."

"Yeah, (the president) doesn't want to do it."

"Well, I don't know how I can agree to your new cost targets."

"That's all right; I'm going to give it to Art."

Deep sigh, deep breath. "OK, what does that mean?"

"You'll find out."

About a month later, in August, about a year into my role, while
I was at Disney World with my family, my boss tracked me down. "I
hate to bother you on your holiday, but…"

John took away the large corporate training groups and gave
them to Art, who was transitioning, just back from a stint in China,
on his way to retirement after a long and respected career. A valuable contributor. I only knew him a little bit, but I liked and trusted
him. He had been so good at cost-cutting in Manufacturing that
they felt he could leverage that capability to squeeze more out of
Training. I went to Toronto to see him and promised to do whatever
I could to help. Then I went to see John because I wanted feedback.
Did I fail? What's the learning in this for me? He said, "No, you did
great. It's just that I want to *outsource* training and Art has had great
results outsourcing. You know, you go work on your knowledge management stuff. That's good stuff; that's OK. Just keep doing that."

I was losing the vast majority of my employees. "John, you're missing the point. If you take away all of training and outsource it, I no longer get the benefit of the cost savings. So how am I supposed to fund the knowledge management stuff?"

He cleverly fed back to me my own words: "You don't have to own it. You always tell me that you shouldn't have to own stuff, that reorganizing is not the answer."

I reacted emotionally to the demise of *my* organization, triggering one of my occasional trips to the amusement park of angst: I felt like I was forever on a roller coaster, an old wooden one, the kind that bangs you around and gives you a headache. I was often on the edge of leaving the company, threatening to quit or asking for a package. This was one of those moments at the bottom of the hill when I didn't think I could take another spin, could not handle another second of air time. We went to all the trouble. We studied this for a year. We told them it would take five years. After one year they take Training away from me? I should leave the company. Adding to my sulk, Kerry, my mentor, sponsor, and friend, left the company, landing a bigger and better job.

My self-assessment was that I got a check-mark for step one, "fixing training." We did what we could do in a year. We took $11 million out, consolidated organizations, and started some networks. The best feedback I could get was: You did a great job; we changed our minds. We want to outsource training. We're outsourcing manufacturing so you shouldn't be upset, you should understand. We'll outsource anything that's not core.

Learning *is core*! That's what they still didn't get. I did get to keep my title, my band, and my perks. Talking to the few of my remaining staff, reexamining the mission, my beliefs, and my life, I succumbed: "Let's find a way to make this work." We could still drive the mission, through influence.

I suggested taking over leadership of the two existing training networks and reforming everything into a "Global Learning Council." Rather than driving continuous improvement in each of the fifty-plus training groups, we needed a *discontinuous change*. When organizations are in periods of disequilibrium, radical changes in the external environment are demanding radical changes in the internal organization, from structure to relationships. It is no longer enough to "improve fit." It is necessary to devise new work, develop new capabilities and new strategies. A complete break with the past may be needed. As defined by David Nadler in his book *Discontinuous Change,* it is change that transforms core aspects of organizations and is more about improvisation than management. John's recharacterization of the industry from short-short to long-long, and the need to transform the culture into a *data* culture signaled a complete break. The Global Learning Council could enable this culture change.

Councils were strategy setting, policy-setting, recognized boards. As I broached it to John, he said, "The only thing I disagree with is calling it a 'Learning Council.'"

"Well, John, I thought I explained to you why it's no longer 'training.' The issues about training in the industrial world…"

He just shook his head. "No! You didn't hear me. Why would you not skip over 'learning?' Your strategy is 'Training' to 'Learning' to 'Knowledge Management.' Leap over learning and drive knowledge." He had been paying more attention than I had given him credit for. The Global Knowledge Council (GKC) was born.

I invited the leaders of the largest training groups, some of whom had been expecting the call and had begun formulating their resistance. At the first meeting, there was palpable fear when I walked into the room. The tenor instantly became reverent and hushed. Smiles were nonexistent. I gave an honest rendition of what I was doing. I felt that authenticity was going to make the difference. I listened carefully to their feedback. My message was, "If you don't think what I'm trying to do is the right stuff, I'll stop. I'm not interested in a hostile takeover. You've been doing great work, but I think I can add some value." At the same time that I was talking, I felt like I could hear them thinking, dreading my presence. I realized that I had become "them." Later I would get feedback that some people thought my authenticity was an act, that I could not be trusted, and that if they spoke up, it would be "career limiting." In this environment, I was afraid I could only get malicious compliance, not much better than sabotage.

I had no choice but to forge ahead. We devised a process for building a *learning strategy*: take a look at the company's business strategy and figure out what capability is needed to *effectively implement* that strategy, figure out what capabilities you have, and look at the gap. Make learning investments in building those capabilities that are most needed to deliver the business strategy, the capabilities that create value for the customer.

People wanted to understand what my role was. I still ran EOL. From a peak of over a hundred people, we were down to an R+D group of about a dozen. I did not run Training, but I did lead the GKC. On the EOL side, a new objective was to get a learning strategist for each strategic business unit. The GKC's mission became, "To develop and implement a knowledge management strategy that significantly improves Nortel's organization effectiveness."

We built on the concept that learning strategy was about building new capabilities. The first new capability we were going to build was "learning strategist." If we can't figure out how to build the learning strategy capability then how were we going to go out and demonstrate that knowledge management and, more important, the competitive advantage you get from knowledge management comes from building new capabilities?

We set a very high standard of what it would take to be a true learning strategist. We went with open positions for months, searching for the right skills. Budget crises hit. At an HR leadership meeting in Toronto, I was accused of sitting on headcount I didn't need. I gave a speech about what a unique set of capabilities we were looking for. My peers rolled their eyes. But the concept was resonating around the world. We recruited from the benchmarkable customer-focused companies, for example, one of our first hires was from Marriott International. We hired learning strategists for Europe and Asia, and a few more in specific product businesses. We began experimenting, learning, and designing as we went along.

The GKC agreed to meet monthly on the phone and face-to-face twice a year. I held the second face-to-face meeting, about nine months into the effort, in Toronto, and asked John Roth to attend. John was superb that day. He won the group over very quickly by demonstrating intimacy with the strategy. He flattered the group, saying, "You people are important to me. But you're driving change and you're going to have barriers. I need you to go out there and fight." He even posed for a picture with us, which appeared in the next issue of *Nortel World*, along with an article[2]. His interest moved some people off the fence. People were seduced by being in the room with the CEO and being able to be in a conversation with him about their function. They agreed to pay more attention to the GKC because it was important to John, and they mustered up some courage to go back into their business systems and fight for the strategy. Sub-teams looked at technology platforms, vendor management, project management, evaluation, certification, resource sharing, suitcase training, global courseware, and a courseware repository.

But I still didn't have the detail vision of how to implement knowledge management. We were stymied. I talked to John and he said, "Forget knowledge management as a program; it has to happen locally, inside businesses." We used the GKC to do some surveying and information gathering to find out what kind of projects in the company looked like knowledge management projects.

The dilemma of KM is that, in addition to training and learning, it crosses a lot of other categories: leadership, alignment, process reengineering, information technology, and culture. In laymen's terms, it is described at a very high level: People know what

---

2 "Council leads training transformation: knowledge council develops strategies for continuous learning," *Nortel World*, November 1998, page 9.

they know; organizations know what other parts of the organization know…and it's not Information Technology (IT). Then when you go and look for implementation, you find IT. When you go to KM conferences, 80 percent of the attendees are IT people. The value of KM needs IT for delivery vehicles, but the capability to produce that value is beyond IT.

We identified some projects that looked like knowledge management projects. They were just happening and I was keeping an eye on them. In an attempt to learn more about implementation, I flew to LA to meet with Ed Lawler, Sue Mohrman and others at the Center for Effective Organizations. They had published a research study called "Building the Framework for Learning Organizations." What they were calling a learning organization was absolutely a framework for knowledge management.

I invited Sue Mohrman to present to the GKC. Part of the framework for knowledge organizations is building communities of practice: formal networks to drive learning. I established a small research lab to work on communities of practice and build internal best practices for learning communities. We issued a frame-breaking white paper. But my staff wanted to administer and establish more communities of practice. I listened carefully, but I pushed back, saying, "No, this would be a mistake. I don't want a corporate group that's in charge of communities of practice. We need to do the research and get the leadership so they spawn spontaneously. We need to shape an environment where that can happen."

Ironically, even as I became frustrated that we were not getting enough done, we were featured in *Knowledge Management* magazine as a company in the forefront[3]. But, other than being fun, it was

3 "Learning By Doing: Organizations discover that hands-on experience produces the most valuable learning," Michael Robin.

clear to me that this role was not sustainable, was definitely not a Band 11 role. I went around and whined a little, told some key clients and line sponsors that I was thinking about leaving the company. They wondered what I was getting so emotional about. Most of them said, "I don't want you to quit the company, but I don't have a job for you." Ian was my white knight, saying, "I have a role for you. Go do this project for me and let's see what happens. You don't need to leave the company. Do this project for a customer. It will take you three to four months, and then we'll figure out how to get you the next job."

Two years into a strategy that I knew would take five to seven years of total focus, I gave up. But, I slipped my values and did not deliver on my entry statement that this would be my last job at Nortel. I now knew the language of co-dependency, and that I was co-dependent and addicted. I had to let go of GKC, transitioning the leadership to a respected customer-training VP. Once again, I helped my staff look for other roles, and we dispersed EOL to the winds. No funeral, no ceremony, lots of private good-byes.

CHAPTER 14

HOUSE RULES

The term multitasking had been coined to refer to the fact that individuals now worked on more than one thing at a time. We do our e-mail while we are on the phone; we place conference calls on mute and conduct side meetings in our office; we surf the Net or create charts while physically present in a meeting. This is multitasking by an individual, as seen at a particular point in time. We also multi-project, if you will, driving multiple initiatives at the same time. As a change agent, I rarely invested myself in the belief that any given intervention or approach was going to be *the one* that changed the culture. Rather, we led many projects, seeking numerous objectives, hopefully synergistically and reinforcing in a systemic way, to steer us to some tipping point that would make the change inevitable.

During the same time that I was leading EOL, I had spurts where I invested a lot of energy into John's leadership forums. During a planning meeting with him for one of these, John offered me yet another concurrent assignment, coaching Dave House, the CEO of Bay Networks. John was so convinced in his belief that the Right Angle Turn demanded a culture shift—that Nortel employees needed to act more like employees from the data world—that he bought a data company to drive the point. Sure, we acquired their product lines, their channels, and their people, but one of the publicly stated reasons that we spent $9 billion to acquire Bay was to acquire the data "culture," in the hopes that it would somehow enter our system as a virus and infect our employees to the point of mutation.

Like sunspots, acquisition strategies flare up periodically. Cisco, like several of our other competitors, was growing through acquisition. We believed that we needed to emulate their strategy. But Cisco was developing the acculturation of acquisitions as a core competence. Our natural immunity—expressed as "NIH Syndrome," if it's not invented here, it can't be any good—hindered us from leveraging the learning. Copying them was futile.

In fact, an HR exec did some research on specific acquisitions that we had made and discovered that we had never met the business case of a single one. When you want to acquire a company, there's a business case you take to the board of directors that says we'll spend this much money and over time that will add this percentage of revenues and earnings. Apparently, it never happened. HR believed that we hadn't met a single acquisition-based business case. In fact, we lost a lot on many of them. There were horror stories. There was more than one example where one of our executives stood in front of a group of acquired employees promising no layoffs, even as the downsizing plans were being drawn up in his office. It was becoming common knowledge, at least among the HR executives, that we were not good at acquiring companies, *even while the pace of acquisitions accelerated.*

John tasked me, "I want you to help Dave House be successful." He had tried to assign me to be a coach a few times before, but I had always refused, reciting my lecture that a coach can't be assigned by a third person. Individuals must choose whether or not they wanted a coach, whether or not they wanted to learn to change. But John respected my relationship with Ian and wanted to see that replicated. Ian had been relatively unique; an executive as an avid, conscious lifelong learner, and the chemistry between us was genuine, not forced. I had met many more executives who did not really want a coach. They were too scared of failure. Several, in one-on-ones, had articulated to me that they thought they had been promoted too fast, too many times. They didn't think they had the capabilities for the next level, *even as they accepted the jobs.* They were afraid that a coach, or any other form of potential assessment, would expose them to be a fraud. This fear was endemic across the executive rank.

In this case, I had foresight through a heads-up from Kerry who was leading a task force on Bay integration as her last assignment: "Dave House is an interesting guy. He's different. He's more like Ian than anybody else at Nortel. You'll like him because he's a learner. He's a listener. He's approachable and personable. He'll never survive here," she laughed. "Because he's so different, he'll never stay beyond his contractual commitment, but your cause might be served by getting him to sponsor your work."

Dave had only been with Bay for two years. Bay itself was the result of a merger of SynOptics Communications and Wellfleet Communications. He had decided that the best thing he could do for the shareholders would be to clean up the detritus from the merger and sell the company. He had been shopping the company to all of the large equipment manufacturers, not just Nortel.

My first reaction to John was to start listing the plethora of initiatives I was working on. He just chuckled and flattered me, "Hey, when I want something done right, I give it to the guy who's busy." How could I say no? After a few conversations with Dave, I encouraged him to take over my organization. He had a title, President, that made the request viable, but he was cautious, albeit kind. "I've heard about you from Ian, and others. John likes you. Kerry likes you. I hear you do good work. But, I don't see me coming in and taking over staff groups as my 'Hello, I'm here.' I don't see a win-win."

At least he was honest, which was quite refreshing. I liked that he gave real-time feedback, about any aspect of work, even things that others might find inconsequential. For example, after I sent him my vision charts and objectives, he asked, "Why do you people in Nortel attach files to e-mails? Write everything in as text, or paste it in as text. I don't have time to open attachments." Many of the Nortel execs still had their admins routinely printing everything.

I told Dave what John and I had talked about. He was pretty upfront saying, "Gosh, I don't know how long I'm going to last here but I'm committed to be here for a while, and I'm committed to do everything I can to help make the company successful. Why don't you coach me for a year and we'll see what success means?"

True to Kerry's prediction, Dave and I hit it off. One of the first things he did to stimulate our bonding was to invite me, along with his head of HR, to his home. It's this forty-acre mountain top estate, complete with a winery, six car bays, a private theatre, a walk-through closet bigger than my first apartment, and a disappearing-edge swimming pool that made it look like you would fall off the side of a cliff if you took a dip. North of San Jose, the main deck looked out over the valley. As the sun set and the stars emerged, the local coyotes serenaded us. I was a little giddy. Around nine thirty, a van delivered the take-out: three prepared meals (two salmons and one chicken, all in standard Styrofoam boxes) that cost $162, without the tip! I think he gave the guy $200. Welcome to California.

We stayed until two o'clock in the morning. During our second, or third, bottle of Merlot, from the vineyard a stones-throw from his deck, he told me about his twenty-two years at Intel, where he ran the Microcomputer Group when it developed the Pentium processor, as well as managing the highly successful "Intel Inside" marketing program. He talked about his relationship with, and admiration for, Andy Grove. How he cashed in his stock options when Intel was in the stratosphere. So he was mega rich, never had to work again if he didn't choose to, and that led us into a discussion about motivation.

"What motivates people at your level if it's no longer the money?"

"It's never about the money for CEOs. It's always about power. Any CEO who tells you differently is kidding himself. We are just seduced by power and the power that comes with money is what we're after, rather than the money itself. The power of running a big company and having all these employees, all these relationships with customers and suppliers and funders. It's invigorating!"

I really got to know him on a personal level. He made it very clear that he was happy to have me as a coach, that he respected me and heard good things about me, and that he was a learner. He knew for him to stay at Nortel would be a shock, but his commitment to the shareholders, customers, and employees that he was going to stay was authentic. In fact, he thought it would be kind of cool to stay, because he believed we had a shot at becoming number one in the industry.

I asked Dave to summarize what he had learned about us during his first six weeks.

"Tim, I'm impressed at the work ethic of Nortel. There's a great spirit here. People work their asses off. That's good. I'm impressed at your technology and product knowledge. There are a lot of smart people here, good labs, and the technology is very impressive. Clearly, I like the customer relationship stuff. When I go see your customers, they seem a lot happier with you than they have been with me. That's the upside of my assessment. The downside is a lot more serious. I have never seen a bigger group of liars in my life. I am astounded that you don't tell each other the truth. At the highest levels of management, you don't tell each other the truth. There's a culture here to lie to each other to protect your turf, to protect your ego, to protect your business, to protect your customer relationships, to protect what...I don't know. But you don't tell each other the truth. 'Yes' doesn't mean 'yes' and 'no' doesn't mean 'no.' There's a massive culture of deception and protection here. That's the biggest problem. The second biggest problem is that you don't have a clue about how to make a decision. Decisions don't hold. You have daylong meetings to make one decision and that decision can be undermined an hour later when the person who didn't like the outcome ignores it. It's not unique; I think it's a problem in many companies. But I think I can help with that. Why don't you ask John what he thinks about my analysis of the culture? I don't know John well enough yet. I don't know if I can sit with him and look him in the eye and tell him the stuff I'm telling you."

"So you want me to be a carrier pigeon."

"Yeah, if you're comfortable with that."

"I'm comfortable with that as a start, but if you're going to help drive change, you're going to have to develop your own relationship with John."

"Yeah, but find out if it's worth my while."

The next morning, he had me meet with his communications prime and some of his HR people. He wanted me to start forming relationships to find out what they had done to help Dave build the culture at Bay. These staff folks were all groupies. They all loved him.

Toward the end of the day, Dave brought in two different chart decks. These comprised his ready-made solution to fix Nortel's culture. One was called "Problem Solving & Decision Making," and the other was called "Straight Talk." The latter was especially interesting because we'd used the same phrase, Straight Talk, about five years earlier. I had helped facilitate a Global Leadership Forum (part of the GE inspired action learning initiatives) to redefine the company's performance management system. A senior marketing executive wanted to call the new one "Straight Talk." He had basically said some of the same things as Dave: "The problem with our system, Tim, is not what codes we use to label people or how we run our process to develop people; it's that we don't tell each other the truth."

"Well, that should be easy to fix," I said, late at night in a dark tavern in Old Montreal.

He just put his arm around me and squeezed me in a friendly bear hug, whispering, "You are so fucking naïve!"

Dave went through his chart decks so I would have awareness about how he might add value[1]. His suggestion was to refine this story, to Nortelize it, through a top-down process, getting feedback and adapting. He would have the senior execs roll it out through the company themselves, not by using staff trainers. He felt it was the executive's role to demonstrate change through his or her own behavior. The ideal was for John to present it to his cabinet. That turned into Dave presenting to John's cabinet, but everyone else agreed to roll it out him or herself. But they couldn't handle it. Most of them asked Dave to do it for them, which he did. Ian, of course, was one of the exceptions. He drove it pretty deep into his organization, announcing that Broadband Networks would follow House Rules. But in most other businesses, the rollout died early, before it could saturate the middle layers. The main impact was to create cynicism, because the employees who got to see it said, "Yeah, duh. Is there any reason we would *not* do this?"

Dave was true to his word and made a real effort to drive change. We met and talked on a regular basis. I had his home number, his cell number; his admin knew who I was and she always connected me or had him call me back. He was very astute, absolutely authentic. Unfortunately, all of his insights and predictions came true.

After the first CEO Forum that the Bay executives attended, I became convinced that he was not going to stay. Nortel culture

---

1 "Have You Been House-Trained?" *Fast Company*, September 30, 1998, Michael Warshaw.

reared its ugly head. A few snipers took the first shots, and no one came to Dave's defense. Behind his back, the hallway and late-night chatter was vicious. The folklore from the other execs was that Dave was incompetent. "Bay's not delivering their numbers; this guy's a flake. He doesn't fit into Nortel. We hope he's leaving when his contract's up." The antibodies rejected the foreign invader as fast as you can flip a digital switch.

The next time I saw John privately, I said, "John, you asked me to coach Dave to make him successful."

"Yeah, how's that going?"

"It's going fine. He's trying hard. He believes in the Problem-Solving/Decision-Making roll out."

"Oh yeah, that's good stuff! You know that I support that?"

"Yeah, I know you wrote the memo that encouraged everyone to do it. But you're not really driving it."

Dave continued just as he always had, trying to roll out the training, trying to make the culture adapt. He stayed true to his values, kept his integrity intact. Before Dave rode off into the sunset, he took the time to teach me a few more things. One of his main concerns was the Board. He said that, in his opinion, the Nortel Board, this predominantly Canadian, predominantly white male board, was reminiscent of how US boards looked in the 1950s. His experience base was that he had been on three boards of his own companies, as well as many others. He gave me examples of antiquated behaviors. He cited, first of all, change management. John wants to change the compensation system. He assigns the two top execs from HR to take ideas around. They go see each board member, one at a time, on the board members' home turf. They put their best suits on and fly here and there and have dinner meetings, spending the better part of a week or two on the road. They run John's idea of a new comp system by them and get feedback. Then they come back to Toronto and put the comp system together with the lowest common denominator that will be rubber-stamped by the board. That's how they're getting change done: what is the lowest common denominator. How can we assure that there is no conflict at the board meeting?

I told Dave about an earlier attempt I had made to try to get conflict into the strategic decision-making process. There was no dialogue in the top group's meetings, no conflict. They looked at charts, had some conversations, and head nodded with the CEO. The pernicious disease of malicious compliance was infectious. I found research that said the best top management groups that *successfully implement* strategy have cognitive conflict in their decision-making meetings[2]. Results suggest that the debate itself improves group performance by formalizing and legitimizing conflict and encouraging critical evaluation. Dialogue, even if heated and intense, can lead to discovery of new alternatives. The absence of it often leads to the perpetuation of the status quo. The paradox is that the dialogue must be *cognitive*, that is, focused on the ideas and content, not *affective*, or emotional and personal. Cognitive conflict, because it examines differences from a critical and logical viewpoint can trigger affective conflict when people disagree. Especially people who distrust each other, or act out of fear, anger or stress or who feel they are constantly vying for power. When the debate becomes personal, political gamesmanship increases and personal friction heats up. This is the reason that many top management teams avoid conflict all together. Unfortunately, decisions then devolve to groupthink and lowest common denominator, and the resistance starts even as the decision is being made.

Dave said, "You're right on. The best boards actually have a lot of conflict. You know Jack Welch? They have some rousing fights. Jack

2   "Distinguishing the Effects of Functional and Dysfunctional Conflict On Strategic Decision Making: Resolving a Paradox for Top Management Teams," Allen C. Amason, Mississippi State University, *Academy of Management Journal*, Volume 39, Number 1, 1996, pp. 123–148.

goes in and argues for what he believes in, but his board pushes back if they disagree. Let me tell you what goes on with the Nortel board meetings. I've been to the board meetings. HR presents the comp change and John gets up and says, 'That sounds like a good idea,' and everyone says, 'yeah.' There's no dialogue. There were two different board members reading the newspaper during the presentation." He looked at me and laughed. "And you're this staff guy down here who thinks he's going to fix this company? You can't change this company until someone gets to the board of directors and says that this behavior is unconscionable and you get a real board of directors. That's the only way you'll drive change. You're a good guy, but you're not going to fix this place. You want hope? Get Ian to be the next CEO. That guy's real. He's your ray of hope. Then tell him to get a new Board. Then tell him to get new staff, new PR, HR, Finance, Legal, and IS heads. These other guys don't know who they are; not one of them is interested in driving culture change."

CHAPTER 15

TIME TO…LEAVE?

At the end of '99, after the departure of several of my most respected sponsors, mentors, and several clients, I started to wonder if I had any more to give. I wasn't being valued, and I was tired to the bone. I convinced myself that I was entitled to a "package," a reward for leaving. These had become so commonplace at the executive level that I would feel I failed if I left without one. I had been asking for one for years, only sometimes in jest, often in total exasperation. I had been whining to a few of my most senior clients. They were sympathetic and Ian pulled me off the ledge. He called me at home on Christmas Eve. He didn't want me stewing over the holidays. He thought I might come back and quit. "You don't need to get out of the company; you just need a great project. I need your help with a customer. We have a real opportunity here and I've already talked to the customer about it, so you can't say no."

He asked me to design a leadership forum for British Telecom. I flew to England and met with the Nortel account team. They enabled my entry and would do the logistics and site plan. I contracted to keep them informed, but I wanted to treat the *customer* as my client. I wanted to work *for* the customer. They were a little nervous at first, but the VP looked me in the eye. "Just let me tell you what homework I've done. Ian says I can trust you and you have absolute integrity. So does…" He named several other executives, mostly North Americans on assignment. He checked with people who knew me, ex-clients, as well as all the HR execs in Europe. "So

I don't know who else to call. Everyone I've called said I could trust you. So I trust you, but I'm anxious…"

"That's cool. But I'm not going to do it if you feel like you need to be my babysitter. I know that we're not supposed to go see a customer unless we bring our account VP, so I won't go if you tell me not to. I'll go home. But I'd like to build my own rapport and win the customer's trust."

With his blessing, I met the BT team, which included the CTO, the CFO, and the executive assistant to the CEO. After a few initial meetings, many of our conversations were by phone; many of our meetings were teleconferences. I guided and spearheaded and cajoled this thing into being. BT people did most of the work on content. The account team was superb on the site work and the logistics. Ian stayed involved, and even John jumped into the fray. One day, we had a rare snowstorm in North Carolina that shut down the airport the evening I was supposed to fly to England. I spent the next day on long calls with various BT representatives. My wife interrupted one of them and said John was on our residence line. He was sanity-checking what I was doing.

It was a landmark event. John and all his cabinet came to it, as did Sir Peter Bonfield, BT's CEO, along with his key staff. The design was pure action learning, workshop mode, with a focus on how Nortel could add value to British Telecom in their attempt to drive change and transform. Unfortunately, the last day started with a London Telegraph article that was unkind to BT. Predictably, this would cause their stock to plummet during the day. Privatized in 1984 and free of all government ownership since 1993, BT was still a primary constituent of the London Stock Exchange. It was the world's fifth largest telecommunications company, employing over 130,000 people. Sir Peter was summoned to 10 Downing Street and his EA said we would have to end at noon sharp, rather than two o'clock. At 7:00 a.m., I had to redesign to take two hours out of the day. A session that was going to start at one, where all the leaders were to come together for an open dialogue, had to be moved up to eleven.

We worked all morning without breaks and I started the dialogue at quarter past eleven. I sat next to Sir Peter, as my final signal that I was working for the customer. I had just met him for five minutes that morning. I never had a direct contract with him; it had all been through his delegates. As the noon hour approached, the dialogue was going strong. I leaned over to Sir Peter and said, "Your EA says we have to end now."

He said, "I'm not due at Downing Street until one. I can get there in ten minutes, so keep it going." He stayed until a quarter to one. This was part of my measure of success. Before he left, he and John did a little ceremony to close the meeting. On his way out, Sir Peter came over and shook my hand, saying, "Thank you. This was tremendous."

I ate lunch with the CTO and the CFO and collected their feedback. "We trusted John Roth in this meeting; we trusted Nortel. This format allowed a dialogue that could never take place in a sales context. Nobody tried to sell us anything all day." For a change, I slept on the flight home, tired and smug. I still had something to add to this company. Ian was right. Focusing on the customer, directly adding value to the customer was absolutely energizing.

But Ian was leaving. Shortly into the new millennium, he announced his retirement. He felt that I should join the corporate marketing group and do this kind of work for other customers. I had a few meetings with the new CMO, but he seemed absolutely uninterested, acknowledging the success of the BT event, but believing it was a unique opportunity.

Back in North America, both Ian and John told me that the event helped fix a relationship problem, helped restore trust. During the course of the year, we closed huge orders from BT, orders that had been at risk. Six months later, at a sales conference, I was having a late-night drink when a few sales VPs sidle up to me, cocktails in hand. Apparently there was now some folklore on the BT event, and they had been wondering about something. "What was your leverage on that? How much did you get?"

"Zero." They were astounded at my stupidity. "You played a role in building a customer relationship. That's what we do for a living. Did you not know how to structure an incentive plan for that project?"

"No, I'm an HR geek. I did this project as a favor to Ian."

They were incredulous. "You didn't even ask! What about after the fact?"

"No, I was just doing my job."

They were disappointed that no one above me put any kind of recognition package together. They thought I should have gotten a million dollars. I could see their respect for me wither and disperse along with the alcohol fumes. In fact, I did not, for a change, believe my own press. I did not think I deserved a commission. But the absurdity sunk deep: at the same meeting I'm getting this feedback that I'm worth a million dollars, I am also struggling to find a real job.

Still, the ride continued and I took one last shot at the next new buzzwords that were going to fix the company: Time to Market (TTM). Ever since John had subsumed BNR into the product businesses, he had been searching for a more streamlined product development process. He wanted to bury the Gate Process that he had helped install years earlier. The software industry used alpha-beta-ship. They build a version of a product, test it with early adopters, and then offer it, even when knowing that they will have to patch it later. Our offerings were too complex for that risk. Somewhere between the highly disciplined and rigorous Gate Process and the speedy alpha-beta-ship was the hybrid we needed. Time to Market was, in fact, just a new name for a process that had been percolating for the better part of a decade. It had survived, in part, because of a succession of name changes, from "Concurrent Engineering"

through "Integrated Product Introduction." There had been a core of fervent zealots who understood that competitive advantage was created on the front end, on the targeted, in-bound marketing intelligence that could shape strategic product development direction, if we listened to it in a structured way, and *if we made investment decisions on it.*

But they attached a lot of process to this belief, a lot of business rules that *must* be followed in order to succeed. By the very nature of appearing too prescriptive, they alienated large segments of their target constituency. Agreements had been reached that the process would be followed, but a year later there was little evidence that it was having any impact. Malicious compliance was in full command. I was asked to take a look at what was holding it up.

After some analysis, I reported that the experts who developed the process were not the right ones to *implement* it. They were too attached, too enamored of the possibilities. Their presentations came across as religious missions. Convert, or else burn in hell. Their imaginations had marginalized them to the brink of irrelevance. Flying under the radar, they had enrolled a few disciples, a few product leaders who had implemented and were getting good business results. None of them, however, wanted to declare causality or attempt to prove that implementing TTM was the *right* thing for others. As we would want out of good business leaders, they just wanted to grow their businesses.

The missionaries had hired some external consultants to help with the miracle conversion, and I had heard some negative buzz about the fact that they were too entrenched. I met with them and, to my astonishment, learned how much further advanced in their thinking they were than us. "It's not about process," they told me. "It's not about tools. Yes, we have developed a world-class set of processes and tools, but they will not be effective if they are not understood and set in a context. A business context."

"Well, what's it about then?"

"It's about leadership!"

I tried my best to get to the common agreement of what the business issue was that TTM was going to solve. During the course of many conversations with many different executives, I kept getting different perspectives: it's about time to value, it's about time to profitability, and it's about time to wealth. It's about redeploying resources. It's about prioritizing investment decisions. Most of these arguments were passive-aggressive tactics intended to convince me that while they supported the concept, they could not take the lead on implementing.

Somewhere between the poles of "it's a worthless program," to "it's a necessary new way of doing business," I settled on my view. It was a business and customer approach to prioritizing R+D investments *and* it was a dynamic process to organize resources, and perhaps most important, to reorganize resources as priorities shifted. Value in knowledge work, as exemplified by the short-short environment of the software industry, is created through innovative approaches to *solutions*. Products are almost beside the point—the goals of many offerings from business-to-business industries are to enable your customers to gain competitive advantage in *their* markets. That was also the key learning I took away from the BT exercise. If there was ever a time for Nortel to fully shift from a technology/product driven company to a market/customer driven company, this was it.

And, at a certain level of corporate consciousness, we knew it. Ever since the 1995 World of Networks vision, we had been talking about selling networks and selling solutions rather than discrete products. The problem was, again, we did not know how to change our culture, to change the basic assumptions that our behaviors were driven by, to align with this vision. A new set of leadership behaviors would be needed to implement all of the wonderful tools and processes that had been developed. Behaviors that truly valued risk taking, truly rewarded meeting commitments, truly developed leaders who assemble teams—fast—and then reassemble the same people into new teams—in a safe, nonthreatening way.

I was asked to take over the *implementation* of TTM. I absolutely had anxiety that I was going to relive the NOM nightmare all over again and wondered if I was doomed to run in an endless loop until I figured out the tipping point to the leadership problem. Furthermore, during my initial study, I had shot myself in the foot, made success all the more difficult, by pledging to the implementation team that I had no desire to wrest the leadership of their work from the current leader. I said what I meant at the time, but as months passed, I began to believe my own press again: if this thing was ever going to be implemented, I might have to be the one to drive it.

Of course, when I was announced in the role, the people on the team who distrusted me believed that that had been my intention all along. I was cast, understandably so, into the lot of other executives as someone who just wants a bigger organization, who just wants to own more resources. Worse, they felt they were on the cusp of success, and I was just going to come in to get credit for what others had done.

I was reporting into Technology, into bosses who believed in the approach, but that reporting confirmed for the rest of the business units that it must be an R+D program, not recognizing that the only way to prioritize development investments would have to be from the customer/market view of the world. Despite too many meetings to count, and countless promises from sales and marketing execs that they were on board, I don't believe we ever influenced executive leadership in any measurable way.

Meanwhile, the CTO, to whom I ultimately reported, was offered a package. He was a free radical genius with a few personality and style quirks. But he had clashed with the dominant paradigm, which had become in my mind, best characterized as style over substance. Wear a nice suit, promise a lot, don't argue in public, and nobody will worry too much. But dress down a little, use crude language, and God forbid, just consistently tell the truth no matter whom it pisses off and all that you deliver might be discounted.

I knew from the nanosecond I heard that he was leaving that TTM was doomed and that I might really be finished this time. I felt that I had become part of the problem. Despite my intentions and the business need, I had allowed TTM to become a program. Furthermore, I had broken commitments to individuals, to staff people who trusted me when I told them that TTM was a safe place to work. Up until weeks before the end, I was still recruiting good people into the team. As I'd counseled numerous executives, it takes a while to build credibility but you can lose it in an instant over a single mistake.

In fact, shortly after the CTO's departure, I had a chance to be reunited with Rod, my most trusted business client, who briefly became my boss. But my enthusiasm was short lived, as shortly thereafter TTM was moved into one of the product lines of business, the president of which sat right around the corner from me. He told me that he supported the cause and that I should just try and implement it in *his* business unit, rather than take on the whole company. That was Thursday. On Friday, I held a teleconference with the team and told them that we were safe and what the strategy would be. On the following Tuesday, the same president called me into his office and told me to lay off my entire team and look for a new job. I can't say that I was stunned, nor can I say that I was surprised. But boy was I emotional. I lost most semblance of professionalism. "I just told my team on Friday that we were safe. You have undermined any credibility that I had left in my career. Why didn't you tell me this last Thursday?"

"I got new numbers over the weekend," he said unapologetically.

"Did you not know you had a tasking coming?" We had, after all, been laying off for the better part of a year.

"I didn't realize how deep my number would be."

I put all of myself for the next few weeks into doing what I could for my staff: Informing them of the reality, helping those who wanted to stay look for work and negotiating the best packages that I could for those who had had enough and wanted to take the opportunity to leave. As usual, there was a handful who wanted to stay but couldn't land jobs and, after buying them a little time, I had to package them anyway. The hardest work I have ever done. For the most part, they were kind to me, caring and nurturing, and worrying about me. I was humbled, as I felt I had betrayed them, but instead of demonizing me, most of them helped me through the emotional churn.

When I talked to John, he was unequivocal. We had let it become a program. There was no energy or passion on his part to let it live. I was personally stymied about what to do next. "Any ideas?"

"Well," he said, "you could always go back to HR. But for the moment, I'd like you to work with [the product president who had just screwed me]. He's not as good as he thinks he is, and I think you could help him. Why don't you help him the way you helped Ian?"

It only took a few direct conversations to discover that he did not want my help. He came across to me as arrogant to the point of believing *all his own press*. During our third conversation, I laid it out, "Look, John is trying to assign me to coach you. I help people learn; I challenge their thinking. You act as if you already know everything you need to know."

He acknowledged my assessment with a head nod, adding, "I think I know how to run this business."

"Then you don't *need* me," I said, merely confirming what he already believed.

He tried to soften the blow. "Look, Tim, you're well respected. But you're an exec, and I have to lay off a number of *business* execs to get to my tasking. I would have to lay off yet another line exec to bring you in, and I don't have any to spare."

I wasn't seen as a business exec or a line exec. I was still, and would always be, a staff exec, despite a few forays into line organizations. As such, I was seen as being of much less value, expendable value.

I talked to a few other clients and got the same story. Nortel was drastically downsizing the number of execs and no one was willing to dump an extra line exec to bring me in. A few asked me to take a voluntary downband of two levels, and they would give me a role as a director. I knew that HR would red circle my comp, and that the move would not drastically affect my income. In just two more years, I would qualify for a full retirement. But I also knew that staying would hurt my pride, erode my ego, and sap whatever energy I had left. I had preached, after watching a number of people flounder around after being downbanded, that we should not allow the practice, that we should be like IBM and others. If you fail in the level of management you reach, you should be out. I was convinced that downbanding did not work, despite a few exceptions. I knew it would not work for me, and I never gave the thought serious consideration.

I talked to John again and told him, "I've learned what I'm going to learn from HR. I'm not going back there again." I named a number of HR people whose values I shared who had been packaged over the years. I was astounded to hear an HR exec, at a General Information Session about an upcoming reduction in force, all but brag that Nortel was world-class at downsizing, that Cisco didn't know how to do it. The sad part is that he was just telling the truth, just reflecting on what he was valued for. We were world-class at putting severance packages together; we could mobilize on a moment's notice and lay off a large group within a week. But is this something to take pride in? "Nortel values operational excellence over change management. All the execs with capabilities like mine are gone. I'm the last one left. I have coached so many execs that when they stopped being valued it was time to leave. I feel like I've stopped being valued."

He didn't argue or disagree. "Well," he laughed, "I'll be leaving soon, too. We've had a great ride." By the nature of my inquiry, the decision made itself.

It took a few weeks' negotiation to finalize the generous, albeit relatively standard, executive separation agreement. During this time, I made a lot of calls to say good-bye to clients, employees, and friends. I was moved by the reaction, receiving many, many voice-mails, phone calls, and e-mails. Many of the senior folks were shocked, one product president telling me that the "true soul of Nortel" was leaving if I left. I was called the "conscience" and "the most trusted exec." Bittersweet feedback, of course. How could someone deemed to be so valuable by so many not be of value to the whole anymore? It didn't matter. I had seen more valuable people than me leave on too many occasions.

My admin helped me pack my office on a weekend, and I slipped out the back, jack. Seventeen years was a long, stressful roller coaster ride. I don't know if there was even an announcement of my departure. So many of us were leaving that protocols were routinely ignored. There certainly was no recognition. Several months later, some of my former staff got together and roasted me at a wonderful bash. I was reminded, once again, how many people I had connected with, how many I had touched, how many still loved me. I began the indoctrination process of reminding myself that that was my purpose, to help others grow, learn, develop, and approach their potential. This business of fixing the company amounted to an arrogant pipedream, and I have convinced myself that I have not failed. During my tenure, I not only learned and grew as a leader, I provided a little insight and guidance along the way to enable others to learn and grow. My time was well spent!

PART 3

LEARNING

CHAPTER 16

"IT'S ABOUT LEADERSHIP, STUPID!"

I had been with BNR for less than six months when they added training to my library responsibilities. I had hired a couple of people and needed to hire a couple more, so they promoted me into management. An organization notice announced my promotion. Nothing else was different on the Monday morning after it came out. I did have a slight awareness that, for the first time in my life, I was now part of the "establishment," part of the problem.

Focusing on my objectives of providing the right services to my client base, I threw bodies at tasks, taking the easy route of converting a few temps. I ran into a lot of issues that I was clueless about how to resolve, so I followed my instincts, got way too deep in the personal lives of my staff, and tried to be a counselor.

Going to HR for advice, I had a session with the Employee Relations manager and one of my troubled staff members. The two of them sat together and cried. At least in the States, BNR was light in offering training for managers, but Northern Telecom was asking all new managers to take a program called Frontline Leadership, offered internally by an external vendor, Zenger-Miller. Stressing the basic principles of management, the course was geared to the manufacturing plant. Most of my peers in the class were dealing with some very fundamental problems like attendance and substance abuse. My issues were more in the realm of the emerging "knowledge worker." I was trying to get people to understand our vision and mission, to formulate and implement strategy, and make independent decisions aligned with all this.

Polling the other managers at BNR, I discovered that the majority of them had never had any formal training in management. They had been promoted because of their functional prowess and field performance. They had been good engineers and good technical support people who had the fortune of being early hires, so when the company needed to grow, they were first up. As one of them characterized it to me, with many of these battlefield promotions, we were "losing a good engineer and gaining a shitty manager."

Rod listened well, added the function of Leadership Development to my responsibilities, and encouraged me to find something to address the need. It was one of the positive, stronger aspects of the culture: "Don't bring problems to your boss; bring solutions." I studied the landscape, took a few American Management Association courses, along with a few others that had been mass marketed. Not overly impressed, I then lucked into the Center for Creative Leadership, right down the road in Greensboro, North Carolina. I started referring people to their public offerings, especially the Leadership Development Program (LDP).

I interviewed LDP participants, asking them what they had learned and what they would do differently as a result of that learning. I was happily surprised at the number of conversations about self, self-awareness, the importance of balance, family, and community. Answers about behavior changes often included words like trust and respect.

Out of this sensibility, we compiled lists of characteristics of good leaders and created tool sets, handbooks, and guides. We introduced four-way feedback and made it mandatory for all managers. Corporate developed a series called Management Leadership Forums (MLF), interactive and experiential.

The first time I facilitated MLF 1, for newly promoted managers, I was surprised at the common values of the participants: they were eager to learn, thirsty for guidance, happy to experiment and share—and angry at how poorly they were being managed. I led several dialogue sessions around the topic of why the senior managers don't behave the way we were teaching. Why were we preaching something different from the reality? We were teaching teamwork, empowerment, and employee development. Managers were practicing control, competition, and delivering results at *any* cost. I encouraged the participants to stop whining, take accountability, go back, and demand to be treated according to the values we were espousing. I even quoted Mahatma Gandhi's, "Be the change that you wish to see in the world." Easier said than done.

It wasn't until I took LDP myself, in 1991, that I realized the magnitude of the difference between managing and leading. *Managing* is often all about control, setting rules, watching for violations, and administering punishment. Fear is a sharp sword. *Leading* is all about motivating others and shaping environments so that all people can achieve their potential. "Trust me," can sound like a dull defense, leaving vulnerabilities exposed. Good leaders don't have to say it. They shape culture by *making meaning.*

Through the associated assessments, I learned a lot about myself: as an introvert, it takes tremendous energy for me to be working through conversations all day long. I didn't trust people until they earned it, whereas the majority of leaders grant trust until it is betrayed. Way too judgmental, I rely on my intuition, and leverage my learning style. My learning curve needs to be steep and I get self-esteem helping others learn and develop.

Strong leaders can actually inspire change, while weak leaders serve only to stifle and devalue. Over the years, I came to the realization that leadership development would have to be the tipping point, the thin edge of the wedge, the leverage that would be needed to transform the culture, which I characterized as "sick," as it was permeated by fear and blaming. A healthy culture would be infused with learning, growth, development, integrity, trust, and respect. Unfortunately, when I told my Canadian boss that "the problem with the company is about leadership, stupid," she thought I was insulting her. The Clinton campaign reference had not yet crossed the border.

Armed with good intentions, many of our efforts suffered from "programitis." A continuous parade of corporate programs invaded the business infrastructure like a wandering virus. We redesigned Performance Management, renaming it *Priorities*. We redesigned Talent Management and Key Resource Development. We built competency models. We tried to emulate GE with Action Learning events called Global Leadership Forums. I led several Future Search conferences, and we even did an Open Space when we reinvented our Information Technology function. We administered some high-level assessments. We brought in engaging experts. I read all of John Kotter's books and many, many books from CCL. I summarized the best books into PowerPoint chart decks, sent them around, and even organized a few book clubs. Three or four times, we thought we had *the solution*, yet we never contracted well enough at the top executive level to get them to take *ownership* of leadership development. Several of the interventions broke down over poor contracting. From the most senior executives, we got lots of head nodding, good budget support, but very little *behavior change*. We couldn't do it *for them*. We tried to facilitate and coach them how to do it. I still don't know, maybe they appeased us because we thought the issue was so urgent; maybe they got it intellectually but it never surpassed the daily business issues in urgency. Again, malicious compliance, the most effective passive-aggressive organizational behavior, crippled the system like an insidious cancer.

After many years of this, I received yet another request to interview the most senior managers to get a snapshot of our leadership strengths and weaknesses. They were saying the *same things* that employees were saying in satisfaction surveys: we work in silos; we worship heroes, not teams; we're too short-term focused; we honor firefighters (there was more than one executive who used the metaphor that they believed some leaders were arsonists—starting fires so they could get credit for putting them out); we lead by intimidation; people are seen as a "cost"; promotions are based on tenure, not ability; we lack diversity.

And every time we talked about one of these conditions, some senior executive would say, "You can't change it overnight; we have to fill the pipeline." For example, seed the lower levels of managers with more diversity, (and leave us alone up here). I heard this exact same quote, ten years apart, from the same executive. It was another form of denial, another way to say, "The problem is below me." The glass ceiling and the color barrier remained all but impenetrable.

In 1995, for the third time in as many years, I was once again asked to survey the executives and get a common view of what we needed to do about leadership development. Not wanting to do any more needs analysis, conduct any more surveys, or interview any more executives, I said, "No! We've studied it enough. We know what the problems are." We gathered some of the work that had been completed in the previous decade by various corporate groups, and we were able to build a stack of primary research reports that stood six feet tall! We had spent at least $40 million on over twenty different programs—and this was just from corporate!

The first stab at summarizing this mountain of data resulted in a one hundred-page paper, practically a doctoral dissertation. I asked one of my staff to simplify and reduce the report to a seven-page chart deck that would pass the stupid test. We pulled out the patterns that had existed over time, the stuff that showed up on every report. It came down to a couple of fundamental threads: lack of trust in management, fear of losing personal power and control, a product-driven mindset and a lack of marketing capability. Some personal things and some business things, but the same concepts over and over again, year after year, report after report.

Turning a company from one that is driven by fear to one that has more positive motivations can happen in rare instances, if a leadership team focuses on it for a long time. The literature was showing that even well structured, expertly designed large-scale organization changes, like implementing Total Quality or Six-Sigma, often take up to ten years to be effective. You don't institute large-scale changes in big companies quarter-by-quarter, incremental program by incremental program. It was much easier to keep studying it.

I became more and more convinced that the only thing that could "fix" Nortel was to create a new leadership *system*, above and beyond a leadership *development* system. Not just better leaders, although that would be a good start, but a whole set of conditions and practices that would work together to foster the emergence of leadership wherever it needed to occur. In Broadband, inspired by CCL's Robert Burnside, we redefined leadership as a *capability*, rather than a place in the hierarchy, and we postulated that *leadership* can occur anywhere and every person has the potential to develop it, and, furthermore, our strategy required that we needed leadership at all levels.

I talked to Steve Kerr, whom Jack Welch announced as one of the country's first chief learning officers. In his book, *Jack*,

Straight from the Gut, Welch explains the importance of his insistence on two characteristics in all his leaders: integrity and boundarylessness; that is, the ability to see beyond organization charts to the whole company. In Nortel, there were too many instances of slipping the first one (for example, I heard from one of our HR VPs that one of our sales reps had been caught red-handed—on videotape no less—stealing a report from a customer, and his bosses did not see why that person needed to be fired); and quite the contrary, we valued and protected our boundaries because they defined our fiefdoms, measured our power. Welch also believed that the main role of senior executives is to *develop the next generation of leaders,* a concept I could never fully sell.

With deregulation, the telecommunications industry had entered a state of turbulence. As data traffic began to surpass voice, markets were being made rapidly. As response, we did some things very well. For example, we set up a business structure that featured regional major account VPs who established excellent connections to the RBOCs, as well as the independents and the rural customers, who were essentially ignored by Lucent. But despite its ongoing success, Nortel still struggled to evolve into a complex and constantly changing system. The back-end, product development, was not leveraging the intelligence from this front-end success. Furthermore, the start-up data companies that we were trying to emulate were developing organizational forms that were self-organizing, self-governing, adaptive, and nonlinear. Having lunch with several former employees who left us to join Cisco was eye-opening, as they inevitably reported: "We really do work in teams. We really are driven to serve the customer. We really are *not* afraid of our boss." It was hard for those of us who remained behind to even imagine.

For most of its history, Nortel had operated in a world of stable, utility-oriented equipment manufacturing, where the sources of order were structure, hierarchy, and position. Decision-making could be slow because the few large customers who bought switching equipment had multiyear, capital-expense decision cycles. The product life was expected to be long and quality extraordinarily high.

John Roth described the need for change as a "Right Angle Turn." He believed that we needed to adopt the culture of the data world, abandoning, in effect, the age-old culture of the "Bell-heads," the traditional telephone company employees from the vast system affectionately known as Ma Bell, the folks who had spent their whole lives in the highly regulated and slow-moving bureaucracy. The old leadership system that Nortel had built over its hundred-year life threatened the very viability of the company.

Leveraging the intelligence from the leadership studies, we tried to take a whole system approach, devising an end-to-end promotion process. We focused on the executive level, describing the attributes and capabilities of successful executives. Any executive getting promoted would get 360-degree feedback against this profile. This would not be a gate, not a deciding factor on the promotion. It would be a development tool.

I thought this was our best shot yet, but despite agreement across the board, within months of announcing implementation, exceptions were being made. I had set up a gate with executive comp: I would get a call if any exec promotion was presented without my knowledge. I began getting weekly heads-up calls. Despite all this work, despite all these agreements, the process was not being implemented. When I challenged these exceptions, all I heard from the HR VPs was, "(My executive) needs *this business* to move forward." When I talked to the senior execs, each defended his or her exception as the *one* that should be allowed. Arguing this point amounted to wasted words, as I could not gain any authority to insist the process be implemented according to design intent. A major opportunity missed. The process fell apart. Without enforcement, it would not be used.

Concurrently, on a parallel track during the same time period, I allowed myself to be seduced into thinking that *I* could be *the* hero, that I could turn the system through my own efforts. In this fantasy, nurtured while exhausted from too many late-night flight delays at the Air Canada gate, I would conclude my tenure by winning the "Spirit of Nortel Award," the highest level of public achievement in the company, which I would accept to a standing ovation, after which I would humbly thank my mentors, sponsors, and, mostly, my staff. The vehicle to this crowning glory would be the executive forum process.

After he became CEO, John called me up, saying, "I want a new way to bring executives together." The tradition that he inherited was called the Senior Management Conference (SMC), a highly orchestrated event to which you got invited if your band or grade was at or above a given level. The SMCs were legendary for their top-shelf external speakers, exorbitant trappings, fancy clothes, and extravagant meals. During Paul Stern's reign as CEO, there was an attempt to emulate what Jack Welch was doing at GE, so the SMCs started to include learning components. The resulting work-shops were coordinated to get predictable outcomes, and to enroll people in the change that the CEO wanted to make.

John said, "I don't want to do the SMC; it's a waste of time and money. If I'm clear about what I want to change, I'll just change it."

"Well, what do you want instead?"

"I'd like to build on the GM Forum stuff that we did. Real working sessions, real decisions. Action plans so that we actually implement!" He was interested in *influencing* rather than *controlling*.

The first CEO Forum was pretty pure in its intent and design. We invited people because of their knowledge and influence. We set out to invite opinion leaders, movers, and shakers; we didn't care what band they were. In reality, though, of the hundred and fifty people who attended, 90 percent were VPs and up. The big change was the 10 percent of middle and first line managers, even a few individual contributors, all of whom were quite flattered to be included.

In his cabinet meetings and in his memos, John said, in effect, "I want new leadership. These people should be empowered to define their topic, appoint their teams, and do their work, and I am going to listen when I get there." Unfortunately, his cabinet was not buying it. In the middle of planning for the second CEO Forum, I had a meeting with one of the product presidents on another topic. In our one-on-one, he asked me, "Why are you wasting our time? Why are you distracting us?"

I was taken aback, saying, "I'm sorry. I need some data."

"You must be pretending, because you know better," he said. "The way that it works here is that John decides everything and tells us what to do, and we do our best to do what John wants. You're now in this dance with all these teams. You're facilitating this process as if you believe there could be some other decision-making process going on. You're getting all these people meeting in all these teams all over the world, spending all this time as if you believe that there's a scintilla of possibility that someone can decide something on their own. Meanwhile we're slipping earnings and this whole CEO Forum stuff is a distraction. I don't just mean the three days. We can come together for three days. If you want to do that and you want it to be better than the last Senior Management Conference, just tell John to invite everyone for three days and have it be white space. Just let us come together. Stop all these teams from doing all this work. Just tell John to write a memo to tell me what he wants me to do, because that's what he wants."

I argued. "No! He really *does* want to listen. He does not have all the answers; if he did he would give them to you as you suggest." That was a big a-ha for me: empowerment is not something that can be given. People are powered, but they have to stand up and take it.

Troubled, I sanity checked with Ian Craig and he said, "Yeah, that's what some of these guys believe."

Without betraying my sources, I had the conversation: "Look, John, there's a belief out there that you know what you want and it would be better if you just told them."

"No, no, no, they have to own it."

He really articulated, verbalized and validated to me that he was building momentum for change. He was continuing a multi-year change effort that Jean Monty had started. He described this change as three large steps: 1.) Refocusing on the customer to the point of delighting the customer (completed by Jean); 2.) Expanding the product portfolio with the capability of building end-to-end networks (in progress, led by him); and 3.) Instilling an entrepreneurial spirit (the work at hand).

"John, the first two steps were easy compared to step three."

I felt that *he* would have to change, *he* would have to manifest new behaviors of leadership to convince people that risk taking was safe, that decisions should be driven down to the level where the knowledge was created, that *all* employees needed to develop leadership behaviors. He wanted to enroll people in the change efforts and thought that running these types of forums was a good way to do it. He told me, "Get them to own it. They are too dependent on me." But I actually sat in one of the president's office for a planning call. He made numbered lists of what John said. Then after the call, he looked at me and said, "Make sure this happens the way John wants it to happen." No dialogue, no input. Yes, we'll own it. That's what John wants us to do.

As mentioned in the preface, at La Costa, the last forum I was involved in, I had coached several execs to tell the truth. The head of Technology, a long-term career Nortel employee, one of the smartest network designers in the world, gets up and expounds: "The market's not as big as marketing is saying it is; I don't believe these numbers." In public, he received cautious, restrained applause. In private, some were commenting that he was no longer seen as a "team player." Within months, he left the company. Shortly after that, the market collapsed; the numbers, as it turned out, weren't real.

In the next chapter, I am going to summarize as much as I think is salient about what I learned and, hopefully, help others learn from our colossal collapse. But I want to state, here and now, why I couldn't fix the company: I was unable to effectively change the *leadership system.* In my opinion, the work that we were driving from OD was pioneering. When we instituted Novations' Four-Way Feedback, for example, it was one of only a half dozen 360-degree feedback tools. Now there are hundreds. When we adapted our Performance Management system to focus more on development than appraisal for compensation, there were very few references to point to. When we were forming the Global Knowledge Council, we were featured in *Knowledge Management* magazine as one of the first companies to do so. When we were building competency models for Change Management and Learning Strategist, I could find no one else that was doing it. Just reading Adam Bryant's *The Corner Office: Indispensable and Unexpected Lessons from CEOs on How to Lead and Succeed* boosts my argument: many of the initiatives and interventions that we were doing as early adopters have become common place.

So what went wrong? Why did we not leverage all this knowledge and experience to become one of those industrial age manufacturers, like IBM, who could successfully transition to a knowledge age, solutions providing company? Maybe, I played too much to my audience. I played to those people with integrity that I trusted, who respected me. I needed that for my own integrity and sanity. I held true to my values, to who I was. But I think that is part of the answer too. I never learned to excel in the old system. Perhaps I should have ordered a couple of $5,000 suits and fought hard to try and become head of HR, to gain the *power* to *control* what I thought needed to happen. Perhaps I needed to learn to market and sell better, to *influence* and *make meaning* to the resisters, to those who got their power from exploiting the old system, instilling and leveraging fear to get ahead. Instead, I referred to them as dinosaurs and expected them to naturally die out.

Fundamentally, I did not develop the *leadership capability* to effectively lead a large-scale organization wide change effort to develop a new leadership system. I can rationalize that I did all I could from a staff role, as an expert consultant, a facilitator and an executive coach. But I never found the key to change the *beliefs* of the line managers that they *must* consider HR processes as mission critical processes, processes that they would need to invest in developing and implementing to the point of gaining competitive advantage out of them. Like a reflection of our overarching market-facing organization model issue, I never found the capability to leverage all of this intelligence that I had gathered, and knowledge that I had accumulated into *companywide processes* to shape a culture and evolve a new leadership system.

CHAPTER 17

LEARNINGS & JUDGMENTS: CLEANING UP AFTER THE ELEPHANTS DANCE

In the early 2000s, the dotcom meltdown triggered a massive telecommunications industry consolidation. For Nortel, it was like making the Right Angle Turn smack into a brick wall. The repercussions were dramatic and quite sad. Within two years of the La Costa celebration, the stock lost over 95 percent of its value, causing untold numbers of individual investors to lose their nest eggs. Market capitalization dropped by almost 98 percent as 65,000 of us employees lost our jobs. The company's status went from most-admired to most-despised.

The market collapse hurt all of our competitors, but most of the larger ones survived, some through mergers, others through adapting strategy to the new environment. As an example of adaptive leadership, let's take a look at Cisco. Nortel was burdened with massive debt, mostly from acquisitions and customer financing. But Cisco, on the other hand, still had a pile of cash and recovered. CEO John Chambers, when asked what distinguished Cisco, talked about customer focus, learning, leadership and the ability to change. He goes on to talk about creating a culture of trust and empowerment: "It's one of the hardest things to grasp, but the more successful a group is, the more you ought to split it up.

In sales, that allows a more focused approach to the customer. It forces you to cover each of the bases in order to achieve your over-all goals. If you have multiple accounts, you can let opportunities slip away and still have what looks like a good year. But then you're leaving room to make your competitors strong. The same thing is true with R+D or other groups.

"Now, this sort of approach only works if you can empower the people who work for you. If your style is top-down and central-ized, you'll get very consistent performance, but you'll also limit growth. If you're talking about keeping up with growth across as many areas as we are, you really have no choice but to empower. That's not only part of our culture. We also have the applications, the network, and the data design to let that occur."[1]

Why was Nortel resistant to change? For a while, success was the problem, the main barrier to change. Success in the industrial age, especially of companies born in the 19th century, could obviate po-tential for success in the 21st century. Industrial companies just be-came too large and were too mired in patriarchal bureaucracies to transform themselves into Knowledge companies. Part of why Cisco's culture was so differentiated is that the company was born just a few decades ago and remains unburdened by an Industrial Age past[2]. But Lou Gerstner taught the elephant to dance, shatter-ing all rationalizations by transforming an Industrial Age manu-facturing company into a Knowledge Age solutions company. It can be done. IBM did it. When you read his book, *Who Says Elephants Can't Dance? Inside IBM's Historic Turnaround*, he makes it sound *easy*: focus on the customer and develop the right leadership model.

1 "John Chambers: After the Deluge," by George Anders, Fast Company, Issue 48, July 2001, page 100

2 Bunnell, David, *Making the Cisco Connection: The Story Behind the Real Internet Superpower*

Was it too late for Nortel to transform? Accounting mishaps notwithstanding, Nortel retained a certain respect in the market for its longevity and for its decades of product excellence. Employee spirit had been beaten down and was flickering, but had not been extinguished. There remained a significant embedded base of Nortel products in large and complex networks. The market also demanded choice: a paucity of vendors would have stifled innovation and driven up cost models. There were less than ten serious contenders with the capability of installing and servicing networks on a global basis. Any company that continued to bring in billions of dollars in revenue had time to learn, even time to transform.

But it wouldn't happen for free, and it couldn't happen just from product excellence or technological prowess. The world was too small, the knowledge too easy to replicate, the products too easy to knock-off. For Nortel to thrive, it would have had to redefine its value proposition the way IBM did. It would have had to become a world leader in leveraging the knowledge it had built up over the previous hundred years. Unfortunately, we let a lot of that intellectual capital walk out the door, and we could never deliver on the vision of becoming a provider of networks and the developer of solutions. Success would have required Nortel to develop new business models for its customers, and for itself; to reignite the motivation of employees to new levels of energy; to win back the faith of the right customers and to win back the trust of the best suppliers. It would have had to develop a new leadership culture, one that valued—and demanded—integrity above all else!

I have seen no evidence that any of the CEOs after I left demonstrated transformative, adaptive, visionary leadership. Unfortunately, they were not expected to: According to Bagnall, in "100 Days," Chairman Red Wilson, in searching for a replacement for John Roth in 2001, said, "The time for visionaries is over[3]." If there was ever a bell sounding a death knell, I think it was at that moment. Frank Dunn, who I know well and respect, was mired in

---

3 Bagnall, *100 Days...* page 30.

accounting issues. History so far has judged that the board fired him prematurely, and the courts absolved him. William Owens stayed just eighteen months. Mike Zafirovski had a reputation as a turnaround specialist. The board must have believed deeply in his capability, given that they agreed to pay $11.5 million to settle a lawsuit brought by Motorola alleging infringement of a noncompete agreement[4]. Filing for bankruptcy might have been the only way to shed the crushing debt. But liquidating a company whose intellectual property eventually sold for over $4.5 billion?

In the previous chapter, I explained that the company needed a whole new leadership system to survive. It did not develop one. As my conclusion, I want to expound on a few of the specific attributes of a leadership system that would have had the potential to crest that elusive tipping point. Above all else, in the Knowledge Age, successful organizations need adaptive leaders who understand that leading change is their most important capability. The leadership system needs to develop, promote, and reward:

LEADERS WHO STAY!

The average CEO tenure during Nortel's last two decades was just a little over three years. It might appear that some of them took the job to further their own careers or to pursue their own agendas. Not one of them behaved in a way that said, "I'll be here as long as it takes."

As a contrast, consider Ray Champ, the CEO of WakeMed in Raleigh, North Carolina, who completed twenty years. He led a multiyear, multifaceted change effort to restore pride. When asked if he ever got discouraged, he said, "Yes, somewhere around the five- or six-year mark, I started to worry that it wasn't taking, and I got a little discouraged." He kept at it for another dozen years after that, transforming the hospital from one that was despised to one

---

4 Vasudev, P. M. "Corporate Governance at Nortel."

that is admired. How did he do it? Through customer focus and leadership development, yes. But he also made a personal commitment that *his* purpose was to fix this hospital. "A true leader is a person with a fairly good dose of humility," Champ explained. "Someone who recognizes those around him really have the best ideas."[5] He just wanted the community to have a better hospital.

Tenure discipline needs to be installed throughout the hierarchy. Center for Creative Leadership research has posited that an ideal development assignment for a leader is a minimum of three years: year one is for learning, year two for trying stuff to improve, and year three for learning the effects of what you did. The one time we were able to measure the average length of management assignments at Nortel, we came up with fourteen months. So the norm became: come in, do stuff, and get out before the shit hits the fan. The culture of blame proliferated. New people in roles believed they had to clean up after the last person; not recognizing that when they left someone would come in and clean up after them. There were instances of bailing out errant leaders, some with serious flaws, by granting packages, buying out the bad behavior. A senior HR exec once told me how proud he was that "we have never lost a major lawsuit." At what cost? Nobody tracked, nobody measured, but the stories became folklore, part of the heritage. Make a commitment to learning by lengthening job assignments; let some of these leaders clean their own stuff up.

LEADERS WHO DEMAND A REAL BOARD!

Reading newspapers during board meetings is unconscionable. Rubber-stamping whatever the CEO wants to do is irresponsible. Allowing HR to schmooze you to your lowest common denominator is just plain lazy. Directors have responsibilities and must be held accountable. Each major decision from the implementation

5 Smith, Rick. "CEO of WakeMed to Retire in July," *Metro Magazine*

of a compensation system that perpetuated a sick culture to the $8 billion acquisition of Bay Networks required board approval. Was Nortel's board asleep or just awash in success? It doesn't matter. In my opinion, they were delinquent and deficient.

When I used to coach executives or, indeed, teach OD people, about mission statements and objective setting, I used to urge audacity. Sometimes, leaders told me that they just wanted to survive, and I used to respond that if survival is your only goal, you probably won't. According to *The Globe and Mail,* as early as 2003, "The main concern of the board was the survival of the company.[6]" Too low a target. As stated earlier, boards must challenge, argue, and make tough decisions. And CEOs must demand boards who do so. Just as you need a high performing work force, you need a high performing board and you must deliberately go about establishing one[7].

LEADERS WHO INSIST ON INTEGRITY IN EVERY ASPECT OF THE BUSINESS MODEL—*EVERY DAY, EVERY DECISION, NO EXCEPTIONS*!

For years, my mantra was Welch's integrity and boundarylessness. Any time I had a moment's opportunity with an executive team, I would preach the same sermon. "Your job is not just to get business results. Your job is to build a sustaining culture, to build the leaders of the future. The higher you go in the organization, the more of your job it should become." Most groups would head nod, as if they agreed, making it that much harder to get them to behave *as if they really did.*

We once had a business unit that was deemed to lack integrity. The leaders were notorious. Even if half the rumors about this business' behavior were false, the *belief* was that they were true. I

---

6   McFarland, Janet. "Nortel board fired CEO after reading investigators' report."

7   For much more on building effective boards, see Jay Conger's *Corporate Boards: New Strategies for Adding Value at the Top*

was asked if I wanted to be the HR person supporting that group and flew in for an interview with the president. After about a half hour, I asked him, "How do you feel about your reputation? Do you care that people say you're evil?"

He didn't blink an eye. "I don't give a shit. I'm here to run a business, not win a popularity contest." I declined the offer. He left a few years later.

As I've mentioned before, the financing of deals led to a lot of pain. We need top line growth, so we find someone who is willing to take our money to buy our equipment, thereby driving up our forecasts and, at the time, our stock price. Many of these customers did not have established business models or track records, and some were never able to pay off these bills. Ethical business practice? Sounds more like the type of behavior that leads to bank bailouts! Integrity issues may not always be obvious but they must be rooted out and dealt with.

LEADERS WHO MANAGE KNOWLEDGE—OR AT LEAST LEARN HOW TO READ!

The lack of any articulated approach to knowledge management or any respect for the value of information is a particularly poignant irony. I was hired as a librarian. We evolved from Information Resource Centers to Learning Resource Centers. We briefly toyed with the idea of the Global Knowledge Council. We manufactured state-of-the-art telecommunications equipment for access to and dissemination of information. Yet, before I left, the decision was made to dissolve the last remnants of the library network.

Gone were the archivists, the organizational historians, and the keepers of the intellectual capital. Organizational memory was suffering from amnesia and the company was doomed to make the same mistakes over and over again. The overreliance on PowerPoint charts and the omnipresence of the laptop computer with its attendant addiction to e-mail, instant messages, and real-time quotes had all combined to infect the whole company. Few leaders kept up with the most basic literature in leading organizations.

I practiced a simple personal habit. I used airplane time for reading books. I didn't do charts, didn't do e-mail, didn't play solitaire. I read books and learned about leveraging your core capabilities—a concept that would have prevented us from losing in business areas that we had inadequate expertise in. I read that most reengineering efforts were failing even as we were starting ours up. I read that there is a discipline and strategy to making acquisitions and merger decisions and an additional discipline and strategy to assuring those decisions are successful. You must know why you are acquiring companies, be it acquiring products, channels, technology, or people. You must study culture and assure that you and the company you acquire can coalesce into something larger. Of course, I read a ton about leadership, change management, complex adaptive systems, chaos theory, future applications of media, the Internet age, the digital age, co-opetition, tipping points, rules of the game, innovation, dilemmas, strategy, competition, and customers. The road ahead and the road behind. I found very few execs to help me learn from all this, to have conversations about potential applications of what I was reading because very few of them were reading. I even received feedback in a performance appraisal that I should not use "hundred-dollar words," and that I was coming across as "too much like an academic." The vast majority of our executives were staying plugged to the grid all the time: doing e-mail, reading internal reports, looking at PowerPoint charts, creating PowerPoint charts, editing PowerPoint charts, and critiquing PowerPoint charts. Some who didn't carry their laptops were carrying briefcases full of paper—their admins printed their e-mail and they went through it, marking it up, and returning it to her to send answers.

Taking a respite from the information deluge is a choice. Doing so on a regular basis is a discipline. It's a discipline that not only keeps one current, but also nurtures a healthy respect for learning and for the application of knowledge. Every one of us, every company out there, makes mistakes. Markets get missed, products are late, features annoy customers, service is late, pricing strategies fail, and people wander around lost, wondering how they can add value, hoping someone will help them out before they get caught. The key is to learn from mistakes, not to make the same ones too many times.

LEADERS WHO VALUE DIVERSITY!

The company had traditionally had a preponderance of Canadian white males at the upper levels. During my tenure, there were never more than one or two females, one or two persons of color. I sat in *hundreds* of executive level meetings. Many, many of them were 100 percent white male. And many of them did not recognize this as a problem!

At La Costa, for the fourth or fifth time during my tenure, data to this effect was shown and a pledge was made to "better understand this data." Bullshit. The data was self-explanatory. One can only assume that the entrenched powers were fine with the situation, which they saw as an issue or a problem, rather than an opportunity.

There was one woman, a brilliant and successful product leader in Broadband Networks. She led with a unique, caring, and nurturing style. Her employees were motivated and committed. Yet, she was ruthless in her business decisions when she had to be. I had lunch with a female executive one time who had a reputation for being unapproachable and uncaring, you know, a "bitch." At least that's what we called women who acted like men. I asked her, "Why do you try to be like them?"

Her answer: "In order to succeed here, a woman has to have a bigger pair of balls than most of the men."

I was disappointed and told her so. "We don't need more men. We need you to be different; we need some women in power." She laughed at my naiveté.

Back at La Costa, during the cocktail hour, I was trying to explain to one of the execs, someone who genuinely seemed perplexed at the data that had been presented earlier, what the data might mean. He was sincere, I think, when he asked me, "Why do women think it's different for them?"

"I don't know," I laughed. "I guess it's because they have to be two or three times better than the men to get promoted to the next level. But that's just my opinion. Let's ask someone else." I called over the female exec in the room and I asked her what she thought, repeating my opinion.

She looked at me with a sly smile, furrowed her brow, and then gave me a skeptical look as if I should know better. "Two or three times better? Two or three?" she repeated. Then she took her eyes off me and slowly turned to the hapless male who had innocently started this discourse and locked on his eyes, as she all but growled, "How about ten *fucking* times better and even then you might not get promoted to the next level? Two or three? Give me a *fucking* break!"

As she walked away, I turned to the exec and said, "Gee, I guess I was wrong."

It was not just gender and color. There was an absolute age bias. I have never been in any other community where they start to write you off as "old" when you turn fifty. The culture encouraged the delivery of black balloons to your office on that milestone. Again, we were all thankful for the generous packages, signing the releases promising that we wouldn't sue, but the result was that there was no respect for accumulated wisdom.

There was no diversity in decision-making, in meeting management, in promotion and other HR processes. Too many leaders would not give bad news; would avoid conflict at all costs. But in private, careers could be destroyed before the employee knew what happened. Diversity of style could be enough to undo a career: "he's a flake," or "she's too moody," could bring the end to a development conversation. "He's a good guy," could get people promoted. Innovation demands diversity of opinion, demands some give and take. Groupthink can maintain the status quo, but it can't change direction or develop new strategy.

I want to close this diversity diatribe, though, on a positive note. I'm a recovering racist. I grew up in 1950s Queens, made famous in the 1970s show *All in the Family,* with its bigoted anti-hero, Archie Bunker. If there was ever a black person (that's not the word we used) on our block, she was there to clean somebody's house and she had better be on the bus back home before it got dark out. I tried to overcome these biases as I had the chance to meet some African Americans in high school and college and get to know them as individuals. But it was not until I met the Reverend C. T. Vivian that I was able to feel, just for a moment, the slightest inkling of what it might be like to be a black person in this society. Just like him. The forceful way in which C. T. conducted the *Race Awareness* training, the impactful way in which he coerced smug white guys to admit some truth and to experience some humiliation and degradation, was a life-changing event for many of us, and I will forever be in his debt[8]. Kudos to Nortel for sponsoring and funding these types of diversity initiatives! Shame on many of the executives for staying above them and not investing *self* into changing the processes and attacking the barriers to get the culture *beyond awareness* and into *valuing differences.*

LEADERS WHO VALUE CORPORATE STAFF!

For a few years, we had a chief administrative officer (CAO), appointed by CEO Jean Monty. I know that Jean meant well, but I

---

8 For more on the legacy of Rev. Vivian, see *Martin Luther King, Jr. on Leadership: Inspiration and Wisdom for Challenging Times,* by Donald T. Phillips. Or, read his brief bio and contact him for a seminar at www.speakersandartists.org/people/revctvivian.

think this was a mistake. The creation of this position signaled to the heads of corporate staff that they were not important enough to report to the CEO. A brilliant CFO left the company during this period. He went on to become the vice-chairman and CFO of the Royal Bank of Canada and was named Canada's CFO of the Year in 2003.

I was asked to facilitate some group process work for this cluster of folks, which included my boss. The CAO proposed a new mental model, that of the professional agency. Not a bad idea, it postulated the importance of a professional services organization that would focus on the delivery of client value. But he tried to impose it *on them,* rather than have it be developed *by them.* It was a futile attempt to try to instill a new culture by decree.

In this climate, the business heads saw corporate staff as comic relief, foils to be toyed with rather than partners to respect. Leaving one of the executive forums, I hitched a ride in a limo with the CFO of one of the product business units. He apologized that he had to take a call and I was an involuntary eavesdropper for the thirty-minute ride to the airport. He was arguing with the corporate CFO about a deal he and his president were trying to cut, a deal that would land a big order if we were willing to finance the whole package. When we arrived at the airport, I overheard him tell his boss, the president, about the resistance from corporate. "I'm supposed to tell you that we're not a bank!" The product president immediately had an emotional, immature tirade about the lack of understanding on the part of corporate about the competitive environment in which he was trying to meet his revenue targets, *"targets imposed by the same guy who's blocking this deal!"* His comments about his peer were derisive, rude, and loudly and absolutely inappropriately uttered in front of me. This type of behavior was commonplace, and in the culture of emulating the boss, it bled throughout the organization.

The chief information officers were always in no-win situations. They were routinely given absolutely conflicting objectives. On the corporate side, the CIO was to manage cost, deliver his budget, and provide a network that never went down. On the client-service delivery side, he was expected to refresh the network with the latest bells and whistles, support all software, even nonstandard stuff that some geek might buy on a whim. He needed a maintenance staff so that prima-donna executives and managers didn't have to learn how to control their own desktops. Naturally, he was expected to provide internal alpha and beta test sites for our products, but he had better not lose dial tone. He was asked to provide expertise in Business Process Reengineering when that was the fix of the month, but he should do so without adding resources or capabilities. At any given time, it was a tossup who the line disrespected more, HR or IS. The blame culture packaged out the heads of these staff groups on a regular basis.

HR was never able to self-actualize during my tenure. I was on no less than six "HR Transition" teams as we were forever tying to redefine the organization, proposing model after model, rethinking the value proposition before giving the prior one a chance to establish itself. Short of true transformation, hierarchical gravity routinely pulled us back. For example, we designed an expert services model, organizing the majority of the population into regional, geographic, functional practices. Business Unit HR, led by vice-presidents assigned to product unit presidents, would be small, strategic partners. These roles were designed to coach and advise on leadership, business strategy, and change management. But they were to be almost individual contributor roles, with only a few staff people in their straight-line organizations. When interventions were needed, be they programs or custom expertise, they would draw on the functional practices, like Employee Relations or OD. All of the executives in HR agreed to this model. But we could never implement according to design-intent.

Some of the significant investment in this flawed effort was on an "HR Competency Model," developed by an internal team using best practices. The model was world-class and ahead of its time. It was intended to build the capabilities that would *impact* the business. Like the leadership model, we developed a full-scale implementation plan that would have used the competencies in our assessment, development, assignment, and promotion decisions. Never happened.

Why not? Well, in large part because the line clients did not expect it to happen. We did not know how to market the concept to them, so that they would actually buy it. "The dog wouldn't eat the dog food." A particular cycle repeated itself: HR is judged too internally focused and disconnected from the business. So, HR appoints a transition team to study the situation and recommend solutions. This takes time and resources away from the business. The team announces an approach, executives debate it for a while, and the function eventually agrees to implement a new model, maybe the one that was needed a year earlier. But the clients are confused by the intent of the new model, don't want to implement if it means *they need to change*, and judges HR to be too internally focused. The music stops and some HR exec finds him or herself without a chair.

For in reality, the manifest behavior demonstrated the most value for operational excellence, the business necessity stuff. Over and over, as some of us in HR pursued the competitive advantage model, the line asked us to just do the basics, do the fundamentals, and do them well. Take care of benefits and provide a staffing machine that we can turn on and off as the business cycles. On the employee relations' side, clean up our shit, thank you very much.

The GM success model articulated that "organizing for effectiveness" was one of the four core capabilities, but few of them recognized the behaviors and skills that it took to excel. As long as they excelled at "driving for results," the rest could be mediocre. There were exceptions, business leaders who recognized that some HR people really did bring a unique capability to the table. These leaders, self-aware and lifelong learners, would be willing to take risks, to trust their employees, to push the envelope on change.

These people "got it," and I had a lot of success in playing a role in helping some of them grow their businesses, or in coaching someone else to do so.

CEO's need to hire *business* leaders, not *functional* leaders. Hire risk-takers, not boss-pleasers. Hire leaders, not managers. Give them clear business objectives and measure them on their ability to bring competitive advantage and add customer value, not on their ability to meet a budget, which should remain a given, not a goal. Hire staff heads who will do what the *business needs* not what the *client wants.*

LEADERS WHO ENCOURAGE DIALOGUE—*AND OUTLAW CHARTS FROM MEETINGS!*

You think I'm kidding? I have asked many execs that have left for other Fortune 500-size companies what they perceive to be the biggest cultural differences from Nortel, and the most oft-quoted item was charts. Charts-r-us! What's wrong with charts, anyway? Well, plenty if you become overly dependent on them.

First of all, the speaker cedes authority to the charts. Watch what happens in any room when the speaker starts showing PowerPoint charts. All the attention goes to the charts. And all the energy often goes out of the room. Communications become 80 percent one-way, two-way at best. Often, the accountability goes to the charts. If an audience member challenges something, speakers often say, well, maybe "they" (secretary, staff, alien?) got the chart wrong. This shuts down the opposition effectively.

Next, charts perpetuate illogical behaviors. When I was still at BNR, I had to cross the street to do a presentation for a Nortel cabinet, to secure some funding for their use of my library services. I called a few of my clients and received the same advice from several: bring good charts, be prepared to use two overhead machines in your presentation and be sure to highlight good stuff with a green marker and bad stuff with a red marker. Style over substance. And they were serious. Sure enough, at the front of the room were two projectors, and I made sure I put generalizations on the left side and accompanying specifics on the right, all appropriately marked up in red and green. I got my funding.

Charts can eat staff time and dollars without adding value to customers. They perpetuate the culture of boss-pleasing. I do not exaggerate when I say that some managers spent more time worrying about their charts than anything else they did. It can be the ultimate time-wasting process for the anal-attentive engineer. I have seen execs spend weeks and weeks on a single chart deck, packing it with data that no one cares about and lengthening it to sizes that will never be shown. It is safe to say that only a very small percentage of charts produced were ever actually shown in a meeting.

If they are all shown, the meeting will be paradoxically useless (for the group as a whole) and productive (for some of the individuals) at the same time. As the speaker drones on and on, waxing on the charts with no one really listening, the participants have more time to use their portable devices. Charts block dialogue, stifle conversations, and prevent conflict. That's why we love them so much.

Finally, the impact that the chart production machine has on the employee population, the ones who have to make the charts, must be considered. The knowledge that most charts never get shown is well entrenched. The behavior of iterating the package over and over again, adding a word here and deleting a comma there can be exhaustive. Often, these folks have other deliverables, some that may even add value to the customer, and the hours and days and weeks that they spend making charts so the boss will think he or she looks good in some meeting is time taken away from those value-adding deliverables. The cost in employee time, computer resources, not to mention the forest of paper destroyed in the process, is rarely measured or even considered.

Run internal meetings without charts. Enable leaders to talk to each other, tell each other the truth, and take accountability and responsibility for their words. Force cognitive conflict into the decision-making meetings. Get away from groupthink. Get far away from wanting to please the boss as a reason for being. Have conversations, and have them without charts. Look each other in the eyes and make commitments.

Be really bold and turn off the smartphones and pads. There was a simple Eastern philosophy mantra in the '60s called "Be Here Now." Learn what it means and practice it.

LEADERS WHO LEARN, TAKE ACCOUNTABILITY, AND RESPECT INDIVIDUALS!

In addition to the tidbit about chart-dependency, the other thing that folks who had left told me that differed at Nortel was around politics. All companies have politics, which is the way individuals and groups obtain and exert power. But people who had gone to other companies reported that the politics were "grown up," business focused, as compared to Nortel where the politics were deemed to be "adolescent or high school at best."

This was a symptom of the fear caused by insecurity. The blame culture had been perpetuated through innumerable downsizings. The quality of people who had been asked to leave is reflected by the successes that many of them have gone on to achieve. In recruiting circles, Nortel was a known talent provider. Blaming others, always finding fault, chokes off learning. Blaming is the avoidance of learning. Nortel epitomized the anti-learning company. I don't have to learn; it's his fault. Blame is self-protective. I'm OK; you're screwed-up. I don't have to take the energy to learn. Finally, again, this fear of being blamed enhanced the fear over affective conflict. If I challenge something, and get called out personally in a meeting as a result, I might get blamed and I might be gone. Better to keep my mouth shut. And the cognitive challenges that might have prevented disaster too often stayed below the surface, below the waves of fear.

I saw it in every business, in every function, at every level, all around the globe. It was an endemic disease that should have been treated systemically. Top leaders must take responsibility for their own behaviors, be accountable for their own outcomes, and not always be looking to can the next staff VP or developing business leader. A leadership system must be based on human values of *dignity* and *respect*. There must be no allowance for behind-the-back shots, personal backstabbing, or undermining. If they act that way, execs are displaying disdain for the very culture that they should be responsible for shaping. How can you thrive, how can you drive positive change if you despise the culture in which you work? If you despise it so much, have the courage to get out of it on your own.

On and off for seventeen years, I, too, complained about the culture, even as I smugly vowed to change it and worked every day to influence it. Each leader must stand up and declare that he or she will not practice those immature behaviors and will not tolerate them in their organization. Period. Case closed. Leaders must recognize that the problem starts with them, *not the layers below them*, and the solutions will have to emanate from them. Solutions will not come from laying the pipe for the future!

Trust people to have their own relationships; do not try to control them through the hierarchy. Eliminate the phrase, "owning people" from the lexicon. Further eliminate the phrase, "owning resources," when what you mean is people. Stop referring to people as resources and start referring to them as people. Stop the perpetuation of the patriarchy. Adults do not need punishing parental units at work. They need coaching; they need feedback and they need learning and development. They do not need to be told what to do, how to think, or how to feel. They certainly do not need to be belittled, blamed, beaten down, or "shot." Productivity comes when you can trust the people who do the work to organize how to do the work. Try shaping an environment in which people can be adults and add value to the customer. Knowledge workers want two things: they want to do valuable work, and they want to be valued for doing so. Get out of their way.

EPILOGUE

The second day of my severance was 9/11, and I was eating a bowl of cereal in my kitchen when the first plane hit the towers. By noon, I had two New York City firefighters in my living room. They had been on a golf weekend in Arizona and were scheduled to land at LaGuardia that fateful morning. Their plane was diverted to Raleigh-Durham, and they called me, the only person they knew in the state of North Carolina. My older brother had been a career firefighter, and I knew these guys through him.

Together, we watched television as the towers fell, even as they worked the phones, only to learn that the "brothers" who had worked their shifts had been killed. We stayed up the better part of the night, trying to imagine how we would cope in this new world. The next morning, we secured a rental car and they made their way to the pile, to dig through the rubble, looking for survivors, finding none.

Worrying about not having a job certainly seemed petty. I welcomed my severance as a gift, allowing me to learn how to breathe differently. Years of living on planes, waking up in hotel rooms, and working seventy and eighty hour weeks had taken a toll. I had been very sickly during those years, suffering through continuous bouts of sinus infections, bronchitis, and fatigue. I was always exhausted, dragging myself through the days.

It was almost a year after I left Nortel before I realized just how burnt out I had been. I discovered health, exercise, good food, the joy of a long walk, and the delight of keeping my feet on the ground for months at a time. I also discovered that I suffered from sleep apnea, a serious condition that was only diagnosed because I had the time to spend a few nights in a sleep clinic, something my wife had been asking me to do for years, but something I never would have taken the time to do if I kept working at the pace expected of executives.

I read Mary Lynn Pulley's *Losing Your Job-Reclaiming Your Soul: Stories of Resilience, Renewal and Hope,* and discovered that I was not unique. In America, *the* conversation starter is always, "What do you do?" Most of us answer by describing our jobs, allowing our work to define who we are. Absent this crutch, I consciously searched for new purpose, reconnecting with my family, actively helping out in my community, and practicing the lost art of reflection.

In his book, *The Corporation: The Pathological Pursuit of Profit and Power,* Joel Bakan examines the institution, rather than individual companies. A legal entity, a corporation is required to put its own self-interest above everything else in its attempt to maximize shareholder wealth. This driving purpose, by definition, opens the door for individual distraction. Most leaders are good people, who do care about the environment and desire to add value to society. Corporations are wealth-creating machines, and in addition to shareholders, they can create wealth for employees, customers, suppliers, and even the communities in which they operate. Even if they once were, they are no longer motivated to do so. They are encouraged, primarily by the demands of the stock markets, to create wealth for the shareholders, *despite the impacts on these other stakeholders.* They are measured by growth, in revenues and earnings, quarter by quarter, not by their ability to add value to society.

A friend of mine, in a similar situation, talked to a therapist, one who had a number of executives as patients. The therapist made the observation that the higher up in the organization an executive climbed, the more isolated he or she became from family, friends, and community. If I had been presented with this data while I was still climbing, I would have gone into immediate denial. But that is only because I had redefined balance and contribution. I paid my taxes. What else did my community want from me? I took a week or two for vacations each year, only dialing into a few teleconferences or flying out for short meetings. I wasn't as bad as some. But I ate dinner alone, a lot, even at least one Valentine's Day, reading my book in an Italian restaurant in London, aware that all the couples around me were looking at me with pity. I missed birthdays, but sent balloons from the road, frightening my son once with a singing clown. I missed meeting a lot of teachers, but my wife did a great job handling that on her own. Rationalizations enabled me to get what little sleep I could steal.

Now, I chalk a lot of it up to inertia. A body will stay in motion unless it is acted upon by an opposing force. When corporations get lucky, and their products sell, the cherished growth propels individuals, and very few forces have the strength to impede. Propulsion is fueled by money and power, yes, but it is also fueled *by the work itself.* There is always so much to do.

I couldn't "fix" Nortel Networks because it wasn't broken. The legal entity was fine. My mission was misguided even as I became seduced and then absorbed by the very culture I was trying to change. I lost who I had been as I became an executive. I didn't see it coming; I would never have predicted it. My rationalizations enabled me to deny it. Yet the alternative eluded me, even as I preached it to others. I needed to fix me. I needed to be self-aware, *not just in the workplace.*

Sadly, Nortel was never able to right itself. Even as the Internet exploded to become a ubiquitous force, as the age of broadband emerged to redefine the worlds of information and entertainment, even as business and social networks grew exponentially,

Nortel stumbled, year after year, filing for bankruptcy and then, almost absurdly, liquidating, creating wealth now only for lawyers. We used an adage one time that, "If we can't change the people, we'll have to change the people." What we meant was if we couldn't fix the culture, couldn't get leadership to learn to behave differently, we would have to get new leaders. Well, after I left they did that. Less than five years after I left, all but one of the most senior executives that I worked with were gone. But the cultural conditioning still ruled. There is a famous psychology experiment in which monkeys are shocked if they try to get a banana from a central perch. Over time, the administrators turned the electricity off. New monkeys were brought in. But, even after generations, when only monkeys were left who had never been shocked, they stayed away from the central perch. From what I could observe, the new leaders kept making decisions much like the old leaders. Even as they ran the company into the ground, the replacements were paid handsomely on their way out, with seven executives getting over $14 million in 2009, after the filing[1]. So, changing the people that way didn't work.

The saddest thing, perhaps, is that Nortel is not unique, not atypical. At the beginning of 2009, when Nortel filed for bankruptcy, the entire Western world was experiencing the biggest recession since the Great Depression of the twentieth century. Financial institutions were collapsing, in large part, because they had lost their way. They had devolved into creating products that had no real pretense to add value to society. The only purpose for those products was to generate money. Unfortunately, most of that money went to people who already had enough by most measures.

Alan Greenspan, the maestro, the former chairman of the US Federal Reserve, professed to be "shocked" by a flaw that he discovered in his life-long belief system: that the self-interest of corporations would drive them to make the best decisions for their

---

1 "Nortel Paid Mike Zafirovski $2.3M When He Resigned," www.billingworld.com/news/2010/03/nortelpaid-mike-zafirovski-2-3m-when-he-resigned.aspx

shareholders. Somewhere, somehow, this aspect, this belief, this tenet of capitalism failed us. As top executive compensation grew out of all proportion to any potential value-add, as boards of directors began to skirt their responsibilities while counting their money, individual leaders began to lose themselves in the allure and seduction of egregious wealth.

Consumers are equally culpable. It took individuals, by the millions, to sign each and every mortgage that wasn't worth the paper it was printed on, to swipe each and every piece of plastic to buy stuff they might never pay for, to cast their vote for politicians that ran the most successful negative television advertising campaigns. To help cope, we flock to gambling casinos, stare at bigger and bigger flat screens, spend the kids' lunch money on lottery tickets and hope, just like the well-intentioned executives, to strike it rich.

So, what is the fundamental learning that needs to come out of all this? Individual human beings brought all this about, making individual decisions. Each of us, as an individual, needs to learn what we can do to help right it. From not buying stuff that we don't need or can't afford, to not dealing with institutions whose values we question, to becoming active in our communities and helping our neighbors, to voting for change: we must grow our self-awareness and develop our purpose. We must stop complaining and do something about it. Those of us who profess to be change agents must continue to proselytize, to teach, to coach, to give power away, to grow and learn. As always, "Be the change you wish to see in the world!"

ACKNOWLEDGMENTS

I want to thank all the people who gave me their time, energy, counseling, feedback, and encouragement to bring this project to fruition. For their deep and detailed analysis in the early stages, thanks to Robert Burnside, Janice Simpson, Ian Craig, Caroline Paoletti, Roger Bushnell, Patrick Dempsey, Jeffery Payne, and Kerry Bessey. Special thanks go to Debbie Morris for her patience in interviewing me, transcribing tapes, and corralling my random stories into a cohesive whole, helping me to get the Broadband story straight. For their guidance in the end stages, I would like to thank John Tyson, Adrian Horwood, Bill Morris, Matt Desch, Michael Rutledge, Karen Tax, Michael Camp, and Kristin Murphy. Finally, for her unending support during all my journeys, my partner for over forty years now, Janis Dempsey.

Book cover design is by Colleen Dempsey. Copyright images used with permission.

BIBLIOGRAPHY

Amason, A.C., Thompson, K. T., Hochwarter, W. A. and Harrison, A. W. "Conflict: An Important dimension in successful management teams," *Organizational Dynamics.* Fall, 23 (2), 1995: 20–34.

Anders, George. "John Chambers: After the Deluge," *Fast Company,* Issue 48, July 2001.

——"Distinguishing the Effects of Functional and Dysfunctional Conflict On Strategic Decision Making: Resolving a Paradox for Top Management Teams," Mississippi State University, *Academy of Management Journal,* Volume 39, Number 1, 1996, pp. 123–148.

Annonymous. "Nortel Innovates, Leads Change." *On Center: News From the Center for Creative Leadership,* 2:3, March, 1999, pages 4-5.

——"Conference Examines Managing Change: Customer Focus and Best Practices Direct Discussions." *Nortel World,* 3:10, December, 1997, page 8.

——"Council Leads Training Transformation: Knowledge Council Develops Strategies for Continuous Learning." *Nortel World,* 4:10, November, 1998, page 9.

——"Global Team Builds Career Management System." *Nortel World,* 4:9, October, 1998, page 8.

——"New Group Begins Learning Transformation: Learning Strategies Refined to Support Business Goals." *Nortel World,* 4:4, may, 1998, page 6.

——"Employees Play Key Role in Performance Reviews." *Northern Telecom Horizon.* December 5, 1991, page 1.

——"LRC Emphasizes Service." *Insight.* 1986, number 5, page 5.

Bagnall, James. "11 Lessons from Nortel's demise." Ottawa: Ottawa Citizen, March 17, 2014.

——*100 Days: The Rush to Judgement that Killed Nortel.* Ottawa: Ottawa Citizen, 2013.

Bridges, William. *Managing Transitions: Making Sense of Life's Changes.* Reading, Mass: Addison-Wesley, 1980.

Bryant, Adam. *The Corner Office: Indispensable and Unexpected Lessons from CEOs on How to Lead and Succeed.* New York; St. Martin's Griffin, 2011.

Blanchard, Kenneth, H, *Leadership and the One Minute Manager: Increasing Effectiveness Through Situational Leadership.* New York: Morrow, c1985.

Bunnell, David, *Making the Cisco Connection: The Story Behind the Real Internet Superpower.* New York: John Wiley & Sons, 2000.

Calof, Jonathan et al. *An Overview of the Demise of Nortel Networks and Key Lessons Learned: Systemic effects in environment, resilience and black-cloud formation.* University of Ottawa, 2014

Clippinger, John Henry III, editor. *The Biology of Business: Decoding the Natural Laws of Enterprise.* San Francisco: Jossey-Bass, 1999.

Collins, Jim and Porras, Jerry I. *Built to Last: Successful Habits of Visionary Companies.* New York: Harper Business, 1994.

Conger, Jay, et al. *Corporate Boards: New Strategies for Adding Value at the Top* San Francisco: Jossey-Bass, 2001.

Dalton, Gene and Thompson, Paul. *Novations: Strategies for Career Management.* Glenview, Ill.: Scott, Foresman & Co., 1986.

Drath, Wilfred. *The Deep Blue Sea: Rethinking the Source of Leadership.* San Francisco: Jossey-Bass, 2001.

Galbraith, Jay R. and Lawler, Edward E. III & Associates. *Organizing for the Future: The New Logic for Managing Complex Organizations.* San Francisco: Jossey-Bass, 1993.

Gladwell, Malcolm. "The Tipping Point." *The New Yorker,* June 3, 1996.

Gerstner, Louis V., Jr., *Who Says Elephants Can't Dance? Inside IBM's Historic Turnaround.* New York: HarperBusiness, 2002.

Gouilart, Francis J. and Kelly, James N. *Transforming the Organization: Reframing Corporate Direction; Restructuring the Company; Revitalizing the Enterprise; Renewing People.* New York: McGraw-Hill, 1995.

Gryskiewicz, Stan. *Positive Turbulence: Developing Climates for Creativity, Innovation and Renewal.* San Francisco: Jossey-Bass, 1993.

Handy, Charles. *Managing the Dream: The Learning Organization.* New York: Gemini Consulting Series on Leadership, 1992.

Hesselbein, Frances et al, editors. *The Community of the Future.* The Drucker Foundation Future Series. San Francisco: Jossey-Bass, 1998.

Hock, Dee. *The Chaordic Organization.* San Francisco: Berrett-Koehler, 1999.

Hurst, David K. *Crisis and Renewal: Meeting the Challenge of Organizational Change.* Cambridge: Harvard Business School Press, 1995.

Katzenbach, Jon R. and Smith, Douglas K. *The Wisdom of Teams: Creating the High-Performance Organization.* Boston: Harvard Business School Press, 1993.

Kochanski, James and Randall, Phillip M. "Rearchitecting the Human Resources Function at Northern Telecom." *Human Resource Management,* 33:2, Summer 1994, 299–315.

Kordupleski, Ray and Simpson, Janice. Randolph, N.J.: Customer Value Management, Inc., 2003.

Koss, W. R. *Six Years that Shook the World: The Story of the Internet, Telecom and Optical Market Revolutions.* Booksurge, 2006.

Kotter, John. *The General Managers.* New York: Free Press, 1982.
——*The Leadership Factor.* New York: Free Press, 1988.

——*A Force for Change: How Leadership Differs from Management.* New York: Free Press, 1990.

——*Corporate Culture and Performance.* New York: Free Press, 1992.

——*The New Rules: How to Succeed in Today's Post-Corporate World.* New York: Free Press, 1995.

——*Leading Change.* Boston: Harvard Business School Press, 1996.

Macdonald, Larry. *Nortel Networks: How Innovation and Vision Created a Network Giant.* Toronto: John Wiley & Sons, 2000.

Maslow, A. H. "A Theory of Human Motivation." *Psychological Review.* 50:4, 370-396, 1940.

McFarland, Janet. "Nortel board fired CEO after reading investigators' report." Toronto: The *Globe and Mail.* June 04, 2012.

——"'Culture of Arrogance' felled telecom giant Nortel, study finds." Toronto: The *Globe and Mail,* March 17, 2014.

McSall, Morgan W. *The Lessons of Experience: How Successful Executives Develop on the Job.* Lexington, Mass: Lexington Books, 1988.

Mohrman, Susan, Albers, Cohen, Susan G., and Mohrman, Allan M., Jr. *Designing Team-Based Organizations: New Forms for Knowledge Work.* San Francisco: Jossey-Bass, 1995.

——et al. *Large Scale Organizational Change*. San Francisco: Jossey-Bass, 1989.

Nadler, David A., Shaw, Robert B., Walton, A. Elise & Associates, *Discontinuous Change: Leading Organizational Transformation*. San Francisco: Jossey-Bass, 1995.

O'Driscoll, Tony, EdD., *Achieving Desired Business Performance: A Framework for Developing Human Performance Technology in Organizations*. Washington, DC: International Society for Performance Improvement, 1999.

Owen, Harrison. *Open Space Technology: A Users Guide. Third Edition*. San Francisco: Berrett-Koehler, 2008.

Pepitone, James S. *Future Training: A Roadmap for Restructuring the Training Function*. Dallas, Texas: AddVantage Learning Press, First Edition, 1995.

Peppers, Don and Rogers, Martha. *The One to One Future: Building Relationships One Customer at a Time*. New York: Doubleday Currency, 1993.

Perry, Lee Tom, Stott, Randall G. and Smallwood, W. Norman. *Real Time Strategy: Improvising Team-Based Planning for a Fast-Changing World*. The Portable MBA Series. New York: John Wiley & Sons, 1993.

Peter, Laurence J. and Hull, Raymond. *The Peter Principle: Why Things Always Go Wrong*. New York: Morrow, 1969.

Phillips, Donald T. *Martin Luther King, Jr. on Leadership: Inspiration and Wisdom for Challenging Times*. New York: Warner Books, 2000.

Ready, Douglas A., editor. *In Charge of Change: Insights into Next Generation Organizations.* Lexington, Mass.: International Consortium for Executive Development Research, 1995.

Robin, Michael. "Learning by Doing: Organizations Discover that Hands-on Experience Produces the Most Valuable Learning." *Knowledge Management Magazine,* March 2000.

Rosenberg, Ron. *Breaking Out of the Change Trap: A Practical Guide for Organizational Change.* Raleigh, North Carolina: Banbury Press, 1998.

Senge, Peter. *The Fifth Discipline: The Art and Practice of the Learning Organization.* New York: Doubleday Currency, 1990.

Smith, Rick. "CEO of WakeMed to Retire in July," *Metro Magazine.* Volume 4, Number 5, June 2003.

Stacey, Ralph. *Complexity and Creativity in Organizations.* San Francisco: Berrett-Koehler, 1996.

Standen, Karyn. "Filling in the Knowledge Gaps: More and More Companies are Getting into the Training Business." *The Ottawa Citizen,* March 6, 1998.

Tichy, Noel M. *The Leadership Engine: How Winning Companies Build Leaders at Every Level.* New York: Harper Business, 1997.

——and Sherman, Stratford. *Control Your Destiny or Someone Else Will: How Jack Welch is Making General Electric the World's Most Competitive Corporation.* New York: Doubleday, 1993.

——and Devanna, Mary Anne. *The Transformational Leader.* New York: John Wiley& Sons, 1986.

Treacy, Michael and Wiersema, Fred. *The Discipline of Market Leaders: Choose Your Customers, Narrow Your Focus, Dominate Your Market*. New York; Perseus Books, 1997.

Tyson, John. *Adventures in Innovation: Inside the Rise and Fall of Nortel*. Ottawa: John F. Tyson, 2014.

Ulrich, David. *Human Resource Champions: The Next Agenda for Adding Value and Delivering Results*. Boston: Harvard Business School Press, 1997.

——and Lake, Dale. *Organizational Capability: Competing from the Inside Out*. New York: John Wiley & Sons, 1990.

Vasudev, P. M. *Corporate Governance at Nortel Board Functions and the Need for Redefinition*. University of Ottawa, 2014.

Weisbord, Marvin R. *Productive Workplaces: Organizing and Managing for Dignity, Meaning and Community*. San Francisco: Jossey-Bass, 1991.

——and Janoff, Sandra. *Future Search: An Action Guide to Finding Common Ground in Organizations and Communities*. San Francisco: Berrett-Koehler, 1995.

——and 35 international coauthors. *Discovering Common Ground: How Future Search Conferences Bring People Together to Achieve Breakthrough Innovation, Empwerment, Shared Vision, and Collaborative Action*. San Francisco: Berrett-Koehler, 1992.

Welch, Jack and Byrne, John A. *Jack: Straight From the Gut*. New York: Warner Books, 2001.

Wheatley, Margaret. *Leadership and the New Sciences: Discovering Order in a Chaotic World.* San Francisco: Berrett-Koehler, 1999.

Whitney, Diana and Troston-Bloom, Amanda. *The Power of Appreciative Inquiry: A Practical Guide to Positive Change.* San Francisco: Berrett-Koehler, 2003.

www.ingramcontent.com/pod-product-compliance
Lightning Source LLC
Chambersburg PA
CBHW051450170526
45166CB00001B/191